*Mangia Pasta!*

ALSO BY MARY ANN ESPOSITO

*What You Knead*

*Celebrations Italian Style: Recipes and Menus for Special Occasions
and Seasons of the Year*

*Nella Cucina: More Italian Cooking from the Host of* Ciao Italia

*Ciao Italia: Traditional Italian Recipes from Family Kitchens*

# Mangia Pasta!

EASY-TO-MAKE RECIPES
FOR COMPANY AND
EVERY DAY

## Mary Ann Esposito

PHOTOGRAPHY BY *Bill Truslow*

William Morrow and Company, Inc. / New York

*For my mother, Louise Florence Saporito,*

*and my aunt, Phoebe Zampini, the best role models anyone could wish for.*

*Thank you for all you have taught me in and out of the kitchen.*

It is the policy of William Morrow and Company, Inc., and its imprints and affiliates, recognizing the importance of preserving what has been written, to print the books we publish on acid-free paper, and we exert our best efforts to that end.

Library of Congress Cataloging-in-Publication Data

Esposito, Mary Ann.

Mangia pasta! / by Mary Ann Esposito ; photography by Bill Truslow. — 1st ed.

p.   cm.

Includes index.

ISBN 0-688-16189-8

1. Cookery (Pasta)   2. Pasta products.   I. Title.

TX809.M17E87   1998

641.8'22—dc21                                                98-22866

CIP

Printed in the United States of America

First Edition

1 2 3 4 5 6 7 8 9 10

BOOK DESIGN BY MADHOUSE STUDIOS

www.williammorrow.com

## Ciao Italia *on the World Wide Web*

It has been nine years since the first episode of *Ciao Italia* aired on public television. In that time, I have met many wonderful people like yourself who have shared with me their love of good, authentically prepared Italian food. We have learned from each other, and I say *mille grazie* to you as well as to my friends and contacts in Italy who have also shared their expertise with me and helped me to extend my experience with Italian foods even further. Because of your interest in the series, *Ciao Italia* has a home on the World Wide Web. To find out more about the series and my books, *Ciao Italia, Nella Cucina, Celebrations Italian Style, What You Knead*, and *Mangia Pasta!*, I invite you to visit the *Ciao Italia* Web site at www.ciaoitalia.com.

# Contents

# Acknowledgments

The people who have worked so hard to produce this book are like family to me; some have worked with me from the beginning when my first book, *Ciao Italia,* was published. I am grateful to all of them for their care and professionalism, their enthusiasm, their talents, and, most of all, for their friendship. They give me great joy. To my dear husband, Guy, my number-one critic and adviser, who gladly ate pasta almost daily while I was testing the recipes; I promise you a steak soon. To Pam Hoenig, my editor, who guided this work with practical wisdom; to photographer Bill Truslow for the exquisite photographs—you have never failed me; to David Nussbaum, who is always a joy to work with, for coordinating the photo shoot with professionalism, and for his acute attention to details, deadlines, and dough; to Marie Pirano for the book cover styling and to food stylist Trish Dahl for the beauty shot styling; to Jane Sutton, prop stylist extraordinaire, who worked right up to the day of knee surgery; to Dana Truslow, who combed supermarkets like a detective looking for the best ingredients; to the team at William Morrow, Paul Fedorko, Naomi Glikman, Carrie Weinberg, Tamara Jenkins, Richard Oriolo, Richard Aquan, and Corinne Alhadeff, and copy editor Estelle Laurence, who were all so very helpful in bringing this book to publication; to Maria Southworth, Jan Enzmann, Andrew Steere, kitchen wizard Shirley Corriher, Janice Walker, and my agent, Michael Jones, Esq. In addition I would like to thank the underwriters of the ninth season of the PBS series *Ciao Italia,* Colavita USA, especially the Profaci family, John Profaci, Sr., and John Profaci, Jr., and also the Sini Fulvi USA Inc. Cheese Company, especially Michele Buster. And to those who make the production of *Ciao Italia* possible, I would like to thank Cynthia Fenneman, the tireless and dedicated executive producer of the series, as well as my "television husband," senior producer Paul Lally, you are the best, and my spokesperson, Leslie Ware, for her support, enthusiasm, and efficiency. Thanks go to John Seath and Glen Gerace at City and Country and to Kitchen Etc., for the loan of kitchenware; to Louis Terramagra for working magic; to my mother, Louise Saporito, who always provides a library of culinary information; to Sharon Amberger at the Anichini Outlet for the loan of beautiful Italian linens; to Brian Agnew, Brian Maxwell, and Penelope Brewster at Ceres Street Bakery; and the Seacoast Science Center. To master wood worker Jesse Ware for the beautiful handmade map of Italy, and to all the readers of my cookbooks and viewers of *Ciao Italia,* thank you for your continued good wishes and support. Without you, the kitchen would surely be closed.

# Introduction

Nothing in Italy so characterizes its universal image as pasta, and even though the Italians do not get the credit for inventing pasta, they certainly get all the kudos for perfecting it and declaring it as their national dish.

Even Giuseppe Garibaldi, Italy's great general and staunch leader in the fight for a united Italy, said, on liberating Naples in 1860, "It will be *maccheroni* [macaroni], I swear to you, that will unite Italy." Since then Italians have been eating Garibaldi's words with abandon with over five hundred types of fresh and dried pastas to be found in the twenty regions of the gastronomic boot.

The importance of pasta in Italy did not come until the sixteenth century in Naples when it was eaten occasionally as a treat or a dessert and meant for the palates of the well to do. What made it special was the cost of transporting durum wheat from Sicily, so it remained a dish for the privileged until the eighteenth and nineteenth centuries when wheat became more affordable for the poorer classes. With the subsequent introduction of kneading machines and brass die plates for extruding shaped pasta, and the development of the art of drying it for longer storage, pasta finally became part of the daily southern Italian diet and remains so today.

This book does not attempt to answer the scholarly question as to how pasta was invented, for that is an exercise in futility. We will never know. Suffice it to say that we are grateful for the invention, accidental or otherwise, which has given the world one of its favorite foods.

Pasta has become the mascot of Italian cooking and it is loved the world over. Its familiarity establishes a common connection; every day, whether in a restaurant or a home setting, the ritual of twirling a forkful of pasta is an action shared by many. Pasta delights us and transports us back to so many phases in our lives: as children we were fed pastina, tiny grains of pasta, floating in hot chicken soup that had the magical ability to cure the common cold (or make us think so) or soothe a raw throat; as teenagers we snacked on cold leftover spaghetti straight out of the refrigerator and declared it our favorite food; as adults we attempted our first lasagne and beamed with confidence and satisfaction, calling it *magnifico*. In truth, no other food has so won the world's heart and praises as much as pasta has.

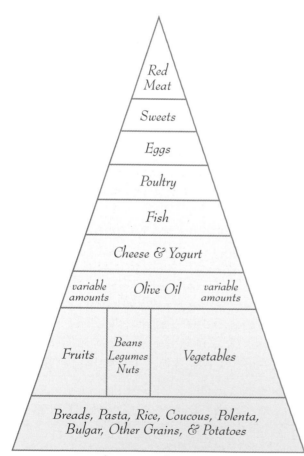

*Italian Food Pyramid*

Why does everyone love pasta? First, it is a familiar food, a comfort food. It is also a cheap food, a versatile and universal food that can entwine itself with and complement just about any other ingredient. It is also a healthy and nutritional food, especially when combined with vegetables, cheese, or fish. Pasta, along with breads and other grains and legumes, makes up the largest part of the Italian food pyramid (left) and nutritional and government health experts in our country have recommended that it be adopted as part of our diet as well.

This book is about making and cooking pasta and introduces the home cook to the preparation of both homemade and commercial dried pasta and demonstrates how to create pasta dishes similar to those that would be served in Italy. Many of the recipes adhere to tradition, like the recipe for pici on page 18, but there are also nontraditional recipes that allow for a creative treatment of pasta, like Salmone, Piselli, e Pasta on page 120.

Luckily we all have access to many good imported Italian pastas. Whenever I am in an *alimentari* (local grocery store) in Italy, I see many familiar names of commercially prepared dried pastas—the same pastas that are available in my own grocery store at home. This book shows you how to properly prepare them.

Making homemade pasta is easier than you may think and the results are so satisfying. Step-by-step technique shots show you the traditional methods of making it still used in Italy, especially in Emilia-Romagna, a region that sets the standard for superior filled and unfilled fresh pasta. And while the fresh pasta we create will not be exactly the same as in Italy because of the differences in flours, water, and even the eggs, it will still be a glorious second choice to authenticity.

The word "pasta" means paste, something made with flour and water, simple ingredients to be sure, but ingredients that must be of superior quality.

For Italians, pasta falls into two major categories: fresh pasta made by hand with unbleached flour and eggs and referred to as *pasta fatta in casa, pasta fatta a mano,* or *pasta fresca,* which is associated with northern Italian cooking; and commercially prepared dried pasta made from hard wheat semolina flour and water, known as *pasta secca* or *pastaciutta,* associated with southern Italian cooking.

The argument has been made so many times by Italian cooks and cookbook authors that it is next to impossible to re-create the flavors of Italian food in the United States. There is much merit to that argument if one considers what is available in the way of authentic Italian ingredients for the American cook. Fortunately we can get authentic Italian products such as *prosciutto di Parma,* and classic cheeses such as Parmigiano-Reggiano and Pecorino, but *mozzarella di bufala* for example (which is flown into the States with a hefty price tag attached), is best consumed on the spot where it is made, in the region of Campania, or its delicate flavor and texture are lost. Specialty food-stores and restaurants are able to fly many ingredients to the States, but time is not kind to perishable foods and for those items that can tolerate some keeping time, the price one has to pay is indeed dear.

Italy's vegetables, fruits, meats, poultry, and fish are also not available to us, although once I was fortunate to have a dish of *spaghetti alle vongole* (spaghetti with clams), the tiny sweet clams having been flown in from Naples that very morning. So we must improvise and adapt our attempts at re-creating Italian flavors. Along with good commercially prepared pasta from Italy, we can also find other hallmark products of Italian cooking in grocery and specialty stores, including quality extra virgin olive oils. One of my favorites is Colavita. Extra virgin means olive oil that comes from the very first pressing of the olives, pits and all, with no heat applied, and contains less than 1 percent oleic acid. Use it in cooking as well as for salads. Fresh herbs in cooking lend authenticity, too, as do the use of fresh garlic and vegetables. Canned vegetables—except for plum tomatoes—dried herbs, minced garlic in jars, and pre-grated, boxed artificial cheese have no place in an Italian kitchen. Why ruin a perfectly good plate of pasta by combining it with imitations of the real thing?

Using fresh, authentic ingredients whenever possible is the key to re-creating Italian flavor in cooking. Re-creating flavor is one thing, but trying to reinvent flavor is not always a good thing and in the case of pasta there has been much abuse. Not too many years ago it was very fashionable to see "designer" types of pasta, including such things as jalapeño pepper pasta and garlic-and-cheese pasta, which flooded the market. These faddish pastas have never had a place in Italian cooking and to this day remain foreign to the Italian palate.

The wonderful thing about pasta is that, like bread, it is one of the most basic of foods, having remained unchanged throughout history, and because of that, what wonderful tastes await you in the preparation of the recipes in this book! Whether your choices are straightforward and plain for any day of the week or delightfully fancy for a special occasion, I hope you will come to the table often to *Mangia Pasta!*

# Making, Cooking, and Serving Pasta

## *Just a Plate of Pasta*

"Serves 8." That is what is usually indicated on a 1-pound package of dried pasta. But let's be truthful, three quarters of a cup of cooked pasta as an individual serving would hardly satisfy many of us, and that is due in part to how we perceive and incorporate pasta into our meals, frequently making it the main course. In contrast, the traditional way to serve it in Italy is as a first course, a *primo piatto,* which sets the tone for the rest of the meal, a parade of small portions of each course meant to be enjoyed in a relaxed, unhurried way.

Italians are very particular about how their pasta is cooked and consumed. There are several rules that need to be adhered to, but the most common ones are:

- Use plenty of boiling water.
- Do not overcook pasta.
- Never rinse cooked pasta.
- Serve pasta as soon as it is cooked.

There is an old expression that "Cooked pasta waits for no man," meaning that when pasta is cooked and sauced, it should not wait another moment before being enjoyed.

I prefer to serve pasta on a large platter or in a shallow bowl, not in a deep bowl. It makes a nice presentation and the ingredients mixed with it are not hidden at the bottom of a bowl. For individual servings, use pasta bowls. I find it easier to eat certain types of pasta like spaghetti, which I entwine on my fork using the sides of the bowl as a bolster. It is easier for children to manage too when there are slippery rigatoni or shells that could easily get away on a flat plate.

Serving pasta with a thick cover of sauce is another common mistake. In Italy, pasta is always lightly and evenly sauced, which provides just the right ratio of sauce to pasta. Sauce should never sit in a pile atop the middle of the pasta. You can always pass sauce separately for those who absolutely have to have a heavy dose. It is interesting to note that in Naples pasta was originally combined with grated cheese or bread crumbs, not tomato sauce, and eaten out of hand, oftentimes on street corners where it was sold. The tomato, a discovery from the New World, was brought to Europe and had not yet caught the attention of the Neapolitans as a culinary food; instead, it was considered an ornamental and poisonous plant and did not come into its own as a sauce for pasta until the nineteenth century.

Cheese is always grated fresh when served with pasta. Fish dishes are never sprinkled with cheese, since there is a taste imbalance between the fish and cheese. It is always best to buy cheese in a wedge and grate it each time you need it. The two predominant grated cheeses used on pasta are Parmigiano-Reggiano and Pecorino. Parmigiano is a cow's milk cheese produced in Emilia-Romagna that is aged a minimum of eighteen to twenty-four months. It must be produced in strict accordance with the guidelines of the Consorzio del Formaggio Parmigiano-Reggiano. Pecorino cheese, made from sheep's milk, is mainly produced in southern Italy. Pecorino cheese has a saltier taste and is the cheese most southern Italian immigrants used when they cooked in their adopted American kitchens.

Do Italians eat leftover pasta? One of the most inventive dishes for leftover pasta is a classic pasta *frittata* (page 91) in which eggs, cheese, and pasta are turned into an omelet, and there are many variations on this theme using whatever leftovers are on hand.

## Essential Tools for Making and Cooking Pasta

The right tools and kitchen gadgets make any cook's job easier and help to guarantee good results. The following list is recommended for making and cooking pasta. Most items can be found in any kitchenware store or see the mail-order section on page 160.

***Cheesecloth.*** Wrap cheeses for grating such as Parmigiano-Reggiano and Pecorino in damp cheesecloth and then tightly in aluminum foil or plastic wrap to preserve freshness.

***Cheese grater.*** A four-sided stainless steel grater with various hole sizes from fine to coarse is easy to use and clean. Using a food processor is not recommended for grating hard cheeses such as Parmigiano-Reggiano because the steel blade can get stuck in the cheese and can also grate the cheese too fine.

***Chitarra.*** A rectangular form with thin, taut wires strung lengthwise that is used for making spaghetti typical of the Abruzzi region of Italy. Available from Italian specialty stores (see mail-order section on page 160).

***Colanders.*** Large basket types with handles are good for draining filled and unfilled pasta.

***Dough scraper.*** A useful tool for scraping up bits of dough from your work surface (see *Ciao Italia* web page to order, *www.ciaoitalia.com*).

***Dowel rods.*** Use wooden rods for hanging and drying spaghetti, fettucine, and other cuts of long, unfilled pasta. Buy varying lengths cut ¼ inch thick.

***Food processor.*** Pasta can be made successfully in a food processor fitted with a metal blade. Use it to make pesto sauces and fillings that require a fine consistency such as for tortellini.

***Knives.*** Stainless steel German makes are best. The ones I use most often are a 10-inch chef's knife, a paring knife, and a slicing knife.

***Ladle.*** Large-bowl-type ladles are useful for serving soups and spreading sauces.

**Lasagne pans.** Invest in glass or metal pans that are at least 13½ × 9 inches. For freezing buy aluminum foil ones.

**Lasagne spatulas.** A wide-faced tool that neatly lifts cut lasagne squares from the serving dish.

**Pasta bowls or soup bowls.** Individual bowls make eating pasta more manageable.

**Pasta fork.** A long-handled fork for stirring and separating pasta once it is put into boiling water. Do not buy wooden forks unless the teeth are securely pegged; those that are glued in will eventually loosen up in the water and fall out. Sturdy plastic ones are a better choice (see *Ciao Italia* web page to order, *www.ciaoitalia.com*).

**Pasta machine.** Look for an imported hand-crank machine from Italy such as the Atlas made by Marcato. Automatic machines are not recommended as they are too time consuming to use, are hard to clean, and the results are not always consistent.

**Pasta machine attachments.** Varying sets of cutters can attach to a standard pasta machine to allow for the cutting of different types of pasta, from fettucine to pappardelle.

**Pasta motor attachment.** A small motor available in most cookware stores replaces the handle of a standard hand-crank pasta machine and eliminates the constant turning of the handle while guiding a sheet of pasta with the other hand through the roller or cutter. The motor has two speed settings.

**Pasta platters.** Large, deep platters are best for mixing and serving cooked pasta.

**Pasta pot.** The best pots are deep and wide rather than tall and narrow, which makes draining the pasta harder. A 7- or 8-quart stainless steel pasta pot with a drainer insert is recommended.

**Pasta scoop.** A fine mesh colander with a handle for retrieving delicate filled pasta from the cooking water.

**Pastry brush.** A useful tool for brushing away dried bits of pasta from the roller and cutter of a pasta machine.

**Pastry wheel.** A small-handled tool with zigzag teeth for cutting strips of pasta dough into various widths and lengths.

**Ravioli form.** An aluminum form for making twelve to twenty-four filled ravioli at one time.

**Ravioli hand stamp.** A small-handled tool with round or square teeth for cutting out ravioli one at a time.

**Rolling pin.** A thin, wooden, handleless pin at least 18 inches in length is best for cutting out sheets of pasta.

**Scale.** For accurate measurements a small kitchen scale is indispensable. Buy one with dual measures in ounces and grams.

**Skimmer.** A long-handled stainless steel spoon with a perforated bowl for scooping delicate filled pasta from the cooking water.

**Wooden work board.** A large, hard maple wooden board at least 3 feet square for making, kneading, and cutting out homemade pasta.

## Pasta Flour

An old Italian cooking manuscript from the fourteenth century cautions cooks to use *fiore di farina* (the flower of the flour) for making pasta. In modern words, only the finest flour was acceptable.

Durum flour is the hardest (meaning it contains the most protein) of all wheat flours, ground from the first wheat to be harvested. It is milled into semolina, the whole grain of durum wheat that is ground into coarse bits for making pasta. Because semolina is high in protein, pasta made from it retains its shape when cooked. In Roman times, the best hard wheat flour, *grano duro*, came from Sicily, which was considered the bread basket of the Roman Empire because its grain was necessary for feeding the Roman troops.

Nutritionally, durum wheat has a protein content of 14 to 16 percent as compared with all-purpose unbleached flour, which averages about 11 percent. In the United States, durum wheat is grown in Minnesota, Montana, Kansas, California, and the Dakotas. Durum flour has a pale yellow color when finely ground and a silky feel and texture. If this flour is difficult to find, use a food processor to grind the coarser semolina until it is reduced to a silkier and finer texture, or see the mail-order section on page 160.

Semolina, a coarser grind of durum wheat, is a deep golden yellow color and is used in the commercial production of dried pasta (*pasta secca*), both short and long cuts. Semolina, along with water, produces a dough that is resilient enough to be passed through a variety of brass die cut plates, which extrude hundreds of different pasta shapes and sizes. Trying to use only semolina to make homemade pasta is nearly impossible since it produces a very stiff dough that is hard to knead. I prefer to combine semolina with unbleached all-purpose flour for making pasta by hand (*Pasta Fatta a Mano*, page 9) or just using unbleached all-purpose flour. Semolina can be bought by mail order (page 160).

Once flour is opened, it should be transferred to airtight containers or bags and stored in the refrigerator to prevent it from becoming rancid. It should be brought to room temperature before using.

All flours do not weigh the same, so it is important to measure accurately when making the dough to ensure that the end result will not be a dough that is either too wet or too dry. For accuracy, invest in a kitchen scale. On average 1 cup of all-purpose flour can weigh between 3.5 and 5 ounces. To measure without a scale, scoop the flour from the bag or container and sprinkle it into a dry-weight measuring cup. Level it at the top with a butter knife. This will give you a more accurate amount than if flour is scooped directly from the bag into the measuring cup, which will compact the flour and give more than what the recipe calls for. Above all, remember that the recipe for dough is only a guide. Other factors, such as the size of the eggs, the humidity in the air, the absorbency of the flour, and how the ingredients are mixed, will all affect the final dough.

## How to Make Pasta in a Fontana

Not too many years ago in Italy it was still required that a woman of marriageable age be proficient at making several kinds of pasta by hand. To do this she had to master the *fontana* method, making pasta in a well, which is also the method used in bread making.

To anyone who has never done this, it may seem a daunting, time-consuming, and old-fashioned method that is not necessary. It is true that the tradition of making pasta by hand is done less frequently in Italian homes now simply for reasons of economics; women are not at home, as in our grandmothers' days, but in the workforce, leaving little time to carry on old culinary traditions. Today women in Italy need only go to the nearest *pastificio* to buy homemade pasta of all types, ready to boil up for the day's meal.

The tradition of making homemade pasta in restaurants in Italy still requires the skilled hands of a woman, the *sfoglina*, who, with deft hands and swift speed, rolls and cuts the *sfoglia* (dough) into its final form.

There is something to be said for making pasta *a mano* (by hand). It truly is a satisfying experience, to make an artisanal product, an individual product, lacking in uniformity, which is, of course, its charm.

I do not make fresh pasta all the time; imported dried pastas from Italy are superior products, and they are part of my everyday cooking. But when I want something special, like filled pasta, that is where I draw the line; no boxed, grocery-shelf filled pasta or frozen filled pasta can compare with the lightness and delicate flavor of fresh. Fresh pasta is made from flour and eggs but in some regions of Italy, like Liguria, water is used for part of the eggs, as well as wine for making the classic trenette (page 19) served with Pesto Sauce (page 64).

Making homemade pasta is not tricky but you should be aware of the factors that will determine the consistency of the dough. The flour should be an unbleached all-purpose flour, not a soft cake flour. I also add some semolina flour (see page 7), which provides additional nutritive value, gives the pasta a golden color, and helps the pasta hold up better during cooking. The next consideration is the eggs; use large eggs, and this gradation varies from place to place. If the eggs are small, you may find yourself using less flour than called for in the basic recipe; you can always add a few teaspoons of water if needed to achieve the right consistency. Other factors to consider are the humidity in the air, which can affect the wetness or dryness of dough, and the way the flour was measured (page 7). Above all, remember that the recipe is only a guide.

Here is the basic recipe and classic method for making pasta using the *fontana* method.

## PASTA FATTA A MANO
# Handmade Pasta

MAKES ABOUT 1¼ POUNDS

2½ cups unbleached all-purpose flour
½ cup semolina flour

1 teaspoon fine sea salt
4 large eggs

Combine the flours and salt and mound on a work surface. With your fist make a hole in the center of the mound. This is the *fontana,* or well. Crack the eggs into the center of the well and beat gently with a fork or your fingers to break up the egg yolks. Using one hand and moving in a clockwise fashion, begin bringing the flour from inside the flour wall into the eggs. Use your other hand to keep the outside of the wall together. If the wall breaks, the eggs will seep out. Continue mixing until a ball of dough is created that is not soupy and holds its shape. Push the excess flour aside and knead the dough until a smooth, soft ball is obtained. Don't worry if you do not use all the flour; adding too much flour will result in a tough dough. On the other hand, if the dough is still sticky, add the remaining flour a little at a time until the

*continued*

desired consistency is obtained. Any leftover flour can be used to dust the sheets of dough when they are cut. Knead the dough until a smooth ball is obtained, then let the dough rest for 30 minutes on a floured surface covered with a bowl or a damp kitchen towel. This will allow the gluten in the dough to relax and allow you to roll it out with ease.

Follow the directions on page 14 for rolling out and cutting the dough.

## Making Fresh Pasta in a Food Processor

There is nothing wrong with speeding up the whole process of making pasta dough by using a food processor. Some cookbooks on the subject instruct you to add the flour first to the bowl of the processor, but I prefer to add and beat the eggs first, then add the flour gradually, which makes for better blending of the ingredients.

*Making homemade pasta using the fontana method*

*Form your flour into a mound, then make a well in the center of it. Place the eggs (and/or any other liquid called for in the specific recipe) in the well.*

*Gradually mixing the flour from the sides of the well into the liquid, being careful not to let the liquid break through the sides.*

*Adding additional flour.*

*You now have a ball of dough that looks like a shaggy mass.*

*Kneading the dough into a smooth ball.*

To make the dough in a food processor, insert the metal blade, add the eggs, and process until smooth. In a bowl, mix the flours and salt together, then add the flour to the eggs a cupful at a time and process until a ball of dough forms and leaves the sides of the bowl clean. If the dough is sticky, add additonal flour a tablespoon at a time and process; if the dough is too dry, add water a tablespoon at a time and process. Remove the dough from the processor once it has achieved the right consistency and knead it on a floured surface for about 5 minutes. Cover as instructed above and let rest.

## How to Cut Fresh Pasta Using a Standard Pasta Machine

I do not own, nor would I care to own, an electric pasta machine that mixes, kneads, and extrudes the dough into various shapes. First, they are very expensive. Second, they are very slow, and third they are hard to clean.

My choice is a stainless steel, hand-crank pasta machine for thinning and cutting dough. Many brands of pasta machines are available in kitchenware stores and through catalog purchase. Mine is an Atlas made in Italy by Marcato. It is roughly 6 inches wide and 6 inches high. A standard hand-crank pasta machine comes with a turn handle for thinning down and cutting the dough, and a table clamp for securely anchoring the pasta machine to the work surface. To make the job of using a pasta machine even easier, the turn handle can be replaced by a small electric motor that fits into the slot that holds the handle. This eliminates the need to manually turn the handle.

These small motors have two speeds, low and high, and are also available in cookware stores or by mail order (page 160).

Pasta dough is thinned by adjusting the number on the knob on the side of the machine, which controls the tightness of the rollers and the thinness of the pasta. There are three options for cutting dough on most standard pasta machines: for fettucine, use the ¼-inch-wide cutter; for vermicelli, use the ⅛-inch-wide cutter; and for lasagne sheets, use the thinnest roller setting, usually number 7. There are also separate cutters that can be purchased and attached to the machine for cutting ravioli and pappardelle.

A hand-crank pasta machine will give many years of service if treated with care. After purchase, follow the manufacturer's directions for setting up your machine. Never immerse the machine in water; instead, wipe it with a hot damp cloth. The first time you use the machine, put a small piece of dough through the roller and cutters to pick up any residue or grease left in the machine from the factory. Discard the piece of dough.

Do not put dough through the machine without flattening it down first with a rolling pin. Thick, unflattened dough can strain the motor and strip the gears. Always lightly flour the piece of dough before putting it through the machine; this will prevent the dough from sticking. Very wet sheets of dough will bunch up and tear apart in the machine, while too dry a sheet of dough will crumble when you put it through the machine. Aim for a balance of damp-dry; you will notice that when the dough is cut into noodles, they separate very easily, and do not stick to one another.

Never use a sharp object like a knife to remove bits of pasta from the roller or cutters, as this could damage or scratch them. Instead, use a clean, dry pastry brush to remove any dried bits of pasta and flour after you are finished with the machine. Store the pasta machine covered in its original box or with a clean cloth over it. Do not put other objects on top of the machine.

# Using a pasta machine to thin and cut the dough

Using a rolling pin to flatten the dough.

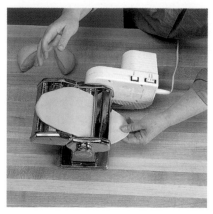

Thinning the dough in a standard pasta machine (fitted with an electric motor)—the second pass.

Thinning the dough in a standard pasta machine (fitted with a motor)—the final pass.

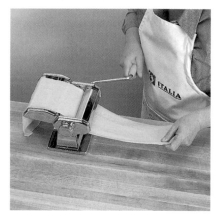

Thinning the dough in a hand-crank machine—the final pass.

Cutting fettucine on the hand-crank machine

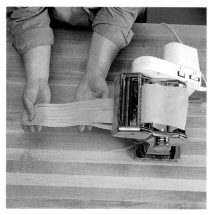

Cutting fettucine on the machine fitted with a motor.

Cutting vermicelli on the machine fitted with a motor.

# Pasta Machine Rescue in Benevento

When I married my husband, Guy, my last name changed from Saporito to Esposito, a very common southern Italian name. Guy's family on his father's side came from Benevento in the region of Campania, but I knew only the relatives who lived on this side of the Atlantic, so when we made our first trip to Italy, we let Maria and Angelo, Guy's cousins in Benevento, know that we were coming for a visit. They were delighted at the news, invited us for lunch, and sent their son Michele to pick us up in Sorrento, about a three-hour drive from their home. The drive past fertile farmlands and large tobacco-growing farms seemed to take forever. Only I spoke some Italian so en route it was up to me to keep the conversation going and Michele was open and talkative and gave us a short history of the area.

It seemed as if all the citizens of Benevento had come to get a glimpse of these "cousins from America" as we pulled up to the gate that surrounded a large stone residence. Holding balloons and waving, Maria, Angelo, and their other three children enveloped us with Italian kisses and squeezes and we reciprocated.

We barely had time to say anything when Maria took me by the arm, ushered me into the bathroom, and told me to wash my hands. It seemed we were going to have lunch pronto!

There were two kitchens in the house, a summer kitchen in the lower part of the house where it was cooler, and a winter kitchen upstairs. I could smell the simmering tomato sauce coming from the summer kitchen where Maria had set a beautiful table with a centerpiece of gorgeous sunny yellow lemons.

Finally we were all *faccia a faccia* (face-to-face) around the table, toasting each other with wine, and being an intimate part of the Esposito family. I knew they were curious about us, but these were my husband's relatives and I was at a loss as to where to begin my Italian conversation.

Maria asked the usual questions about children, where we lived, what kinds of jobs we had, but she really surprised us when she said she could certainly believe that I was from an Italian family with my Neapolitan and Sicilian features, but she was not sure about Guy—her own relative—who she exclaimed was much too fair-looking to be an Esposito!

Her pasta machine saved the moment. I spotted it on Maria's counter; it was an automatic machine, one of those expensive types, where all you have to do is push a button and all the ingredients blend together to extrude different shaped pastas. You never had to touch the dough.

Here was a subject that I was a bit more familiar with. I asked Maria if she liked her pasta machine. *"Non mi piace"* (I don't like it), she emphatically declared. She had tried to break away from her traditional way of making pasta by hand, the way her mother had taught her, in the *fontana*, but it was no use; the machine was too slow, the pasta was too thick, the parts of the machine too hard to clean, and common sense finally dictated that the best pasta could only be made *sempre a mano* (always by hand). And with that announcement came the first course of homemade spaghetti with pungent, black as midnight olives and tomato sauce made from Maria's own garden tomatoes. We twirled it on our forks, savoring every bite and felt right at home. The spaghetti was feather-light and when Guy asked for a second helping, Maria beamed with delight and knew for sure that he was definitely an Esposito.

## How to Roll Out and Cut Pasta by Hand

Before the days of the pasta machine, sheets of dough were rolled out and cut by hand to make, among other types, linguine, fettucine, lasagne strips, irregular triangles called maltagliati, ravioli, little stuffed hats called cappelletti, and tortellini, said to resemble the belly button of Venus.

In my own kitchen, I still use the long, thin wooden rolling pin (*matterello*) that belonged to my Grandmother Saporito for flattening and rolling out dough and I also use her wooden *chitarra* for cutting pasta into spaghetti or little squares for soup called *quadrucci* (see page 160 for *chitarra* sources). These traditional ways of making pasta are fast disappearing; I cherish them as part of my heritage and practice the techniques often to preserve them.

A wide wood work surface is my preference for making and cutting pasta. In the old days a special wooden board was placed on the kitchen table for making pasta using the traditional *fontana* method of mounding a wall of flour on the board and cracking the eggs into the center (page 10). Making a dough by hand required the intuitiveness that came only with the experience of knowing just when the consistency of the dough was right; it had to be soft but not sticky and hand-kneaded into a ball of smoothness. The dough then rested under a bowl for at least 30 minutes to relax the gluten and make it easier to roll.

In Italy, it is amazing how quickly a large chunk of pasta dough can be rolled out to typing paper thinness, the mechanics of which are seemingly effortless for those skilled in making pasta. I have watched Italian cooks roll a small piece of dough out so thin that it covered the entire surface of a large round table. And it made me recall the words of my own grandmother, who insisted that the dough must be rolled "as thin as a dime."

Knowing my own limits in the kitchen, I take a more manageable approach when manually rolling out the dough. I work with small pieces, usually 4 ounces, and roll the dough into a 14 × 16-inch rectangle that is about 1/16 inch thick. Thin the dough starting from the center and roll outward toward the edges, giving the dough a quarter turn each time you roll it to make sure that the sheet maintains an even thickness.

When the sheet of dough is the desired size, let it dry slightly on the board or over a wooden dowel rod. Be careful not to let it get brittle or it will crack and crumble when it is cut. The dough should be damp-dry; if it is too wet, the pasta will stick together. Lightly brush the surface of the dough with flour, then roll it up loosely from one end as if you were rolling up a newspaper. (Another method of hand cutting is to fold the pasta sheet in thirds like a business letter and then cut it into desired widths.) Trim the ends with a sharp knife so that they are even. Cut the sheet crosswise into 1/4-inch-wide strips for fettucine, or 1/8-inch-wide strips for linguine. Shake the noodles out and hang them over dowel rods to dry or place them on clean kitchen towels. For pappardelle, cut 1- to 1/2-inch-wide strips and place on towel-lined baking sheets. For lasagne or cannelloni cut 5½ × 5-inch pieces and place them on towels as they are cut. Or cut the dough into whatever widths you wish. For some types of filled pasta, like the *Cannelloni All'Erbe di Prezzemolo e Basilico* on page 126, the dough should be rolled a little thicker to prevent the filling from breaking through the dough, but not so thick that the pasta has a chewy consistency.

Allow the pasta to dry about 20 minutes if cooking immediately. Otherwise, it can be dried completely for future use (see page 16).

A general rule for stuffed pasta is to fill the dough as soon as it is cut, otherwise if it begins to dry out, it will be difficult at best to seal the dough. Cook the pasta following the instructions on page 29.

# Rolling out and cutting the dough by hand

Ball of dough ready for flattening.

Rolling out the dough.

Rolling out the dough.

Brushing the damp-dry sheet of dough lightly with flour

Rolling the sheet of dough.

Cutting the roll crosswise.

Shaking out the noodles and placing them on a clean kitchen towel to dry.

Cutting a sheet of dough for lasagne.

Cutting a sheet of dough for pappardelle.

## Drying and Storing Fresh Pasta

On the day that I plan to make fresh pasta, I make enough to dry and save for future use. To do this, invest in some inexpensive wooden dowel rods from the hardware store. Buy rods that are about ¼ inch in diameter and 4 feet long. These can be positioned between the crest rails of two chairs and held in place with tape so they do not slide. Place clean newspaper on the floor between the chairs to catch any pasta that falls as it dries.

As you cut the sheets of pasta, hang the noodles over the dowel rods, spacing them about ¼ inch apart. Let the noodles dry until they are brittle. A good indication that they have dried sufficiently is a slight curling at the end of the noodles.

Thoroughly dried pasta is very fragile and removing the noodles so they do not break takes a little practice. First, remove the tape holding the dowel rod in place. Have a large sheet of aluminum foil ready. Carefully lift the dowel rod and, starting at one end of the rod, slide the pasta onto the aluminum foil. Do not crowd more onto a sheet of foil than is necessary. Do not worry if some pieces fall on the newspaper; pick them up and add them to the rest. Gently crimp the foil closed and store the pasta in a cool place away from objects that can fall on it or crush it. Dried pasta will keep for 6 months or longer if properly stored. And because there is no longer any moisture left in the dough, it will not get moldy. Some people like to freeze fresh unfilled pasta in plastic bags. I do not subscribe to this practice because pasta can pick up freezer burn, unwanted odors, and ice crystals, and is difficult to cook correctly once added to boiling water because frozen pasta reduces the water temperature and by the time the water re-boils the pasta is overcooked and mushy.

I often give dried pasta that I have made as a gift. To do this, wrap the pasta in a large sheet of cellophane, tie the ends with ribbon, enclose the recipe for your best sauce, and you have a special gift. Sometimes, for a more dramatic effect, I purchase long-stemmed rose boxes from my local florist; they are perfect for long cuts of spaghetti, fettucine, pici, and vermicelli.

*lletti • bucatini • capellini • ditalini • farfalle • fettucine • fregola • fusilli • lasagne • linguine • malta*

# What's in a Name?

Identifying different cuts of pasta, both fresh and dried, can be an amusing dilemma for the pastaphile since there are about four hundred names for both fresh and dried pastas. It used to be enough to call pasta "macaroni," which in my growing up years encompassed everything from *acini* (grape seeds) to *ziti* (bridegrooms), but as the popularity and exportation of pasta grew, so did the development of regional pasta dishes with their specific names.

The Italians have such natural and artistic flair for everything they do, so why should they overlook their beloved pasta? They have given very definite names to pasta shapes, both plain and fancy. Some of these

*lletti • bucatini • capellini • ditalini • farfalle • fettucine • fregola • fusilli • lasagne • linguine • malta*

shapes are available only in Italy since there are so many artisanal varieties that are locally produced and known only in their locales. Whenever I am in Italy, I make it a point to bring home the locally produced dried pasta of the region.

The shape of pasta determines what type of sauce will be paired with it. Chunky short-cuts go well with heavier sauces that cling to and are trapped by the lines and grooves of such cuts as rigatoni, fusilli, and conchiglie. Thinner and longer cuts such as linguine go better with smoother sauces such as fresh tomato, clam, or cream-based sauces.

For the purposes of this book, I have included the more popular types that would be available here in grocery stores or Italian specialty stores. They include the following, many of which have more than one name.

**Anelletti:** little rings used in soup

**Bucatini:** thick-cut spaghetti with a hole; also called perciatelli

**Cappelletti:** little hats of meat-filled dough traditionally served in capon broth

**Capellini (capelli di angeli):** angel hair—very thin spaghetti

**Conchiglie:** shell-shaped pasta sometimes called gnocchi

**Ditalini (tubetti):** little thimbles of very short-cut hollow pasta used for soup

**Farfalle:** butterfly-shaped pasta; sometimes called bow ties

**Farfallone:** large butterfly pasta

**Fettucine (tagliatelle):** ribbon noodles usually about 1/4 inch wide

**Fregola:** Sardinian semolina (little grains) used in soups

**Fusilli (spirale):** twisted shape; corkscrews

**Garganelli:** grooved pasta similar to penne and a specialty of Emilia-Romagna

**Lasagne:** wide sheets of pasta served with a ragù

**Linguine (tagliolini):** thin spaghetti

**Malloreddus:** gnocchi-shaped pasta from Sardinia

**Maltagliati:** badly cut or randomly cut triangular noodles, usually used in soup

**Orecchiette:** "little ears," a regional pasta from Puglia

**Orzo:** small barley pasta most often used in soup

**Pappardelle:** wide noodles usually teamed with wild boar or hare sauce

**Pastina:** tiny pasta used in soup

**Pettole:** a wide noodle similar to pappardelle from Caserta, but made only with flour and water

**Penne (mostaccioli):** pen- or mustache-shaped pasta

**Penne rigate:** pen- or mustache-shaped pasta with ridges

**Pennette:** tiny penne

**Pici:** thin spaghetti from Tuscany

**Pipe rigate:** pipe-shaped pasta with ridges

**Quadrucci:** small squares of pasta used in soup

**Radiatore:** radiator-shaped pasta

**Ravioli (tortelli):** stuffed squares or half moons

**Rigatoni:** ridged tubular pasta

**Rotelle:** small wheels

**Ruote:** wheel-shaped pasta

**Spaghetti:** strings

**Spaghettini:** thin strings

**Stelline:** small stars used in soup

**Tagliatelle:** similar to fettucine

**Tortelli (ravioli):** stuffed fresh pasta

**Tortellini:** small filled pasta used in soup

**Tortelloni:** large ravioli usually stuffed with cheese, pumpkin, or herbs

**Trenette (bavette):** similar to fettucine and a specialty of Liguria

**Tubetti (ditalini):** small tubular or thimble-shaped soup pasta

**Ziti:** short or long hollow pasta

## Other Fresh Pastas

Many tourists make San Gimignano a destination in Tuscany to see the remaining defensive towers that jut out against the skyline. They are looming reminders of a time when they served as indicators of the wealth of their owners and stood as mighty fortresses against the enemies of the town.

Unfortunately, commercialism has turned San Gimignano into a boutique town with shop after shop of trinkets. After an afternoon of visiting the Duomo (cathedral) and the Piazza Cisterna, I headed to Ristorante Dorando' on Vicolo dell'Oro 2, a small, intimate place with vaulted ceilings and fourteenth-century stone walls. The cooking reflects diligently researched dishes from Etruscan, medieval, and Renaissance writings that gave rise to Tuscan cuisine.

One of the special pasta dishes from antiquity is pici, a thin spaghetti made only with flour and water that the Etruscans from the nearby town of Chiusi served with olive oil, crushed garlic, walnuts, and fresh mint. Another excellent sauce for this pasta is *Salsa di Oliva* (Olive Sauce) on page 59. Tuscan cooks use a wooden rolling pin with grooves to cut the dough, which is a little thicker than for fettucine, into thin strands. The fettucine cutter or vermicelli cutter on a standard pasta machine is a good substitute. This dough is soft and stretchy and it can be made in no time at all in a food processor.

I have given you two versions of the dough; the first is made with unbleached all-purpose flour and the second with finely ground durum semolina flour, which gives a yellower tone to the dough and nutritionally has a higher protein content. Follow the directions below for either flour.

## Pici

MAKES 1¼ POUNDS

3 cups unbleached all-purpose flour (for pici #1) or 2½ cups finely ground durum semolina flour (for pici #2), plus additional if needed

1 teaspoon salt

1 cup warm filtered water

1 teaspoon extra virgin olive oil

Place the flour and salt in the bowl of a food processor fitted with the steel blade and whirl the mixture to blend. With the motor running, slowly pour the water through the feed tube. Add the olive oil and continue processing until a ball of dough is formed that is moist and holds together. If the dough seems too dry, add a few drops of water and pulse.

Gather up the dough and knead it for a few minutes on a wooden surface, adding a little flour only if the dough is sticking to your hands. Cover the dough with a bowl and let it rest for 30 minutes.

Divide the dough into quarters and work with one piece of dough at a time; keep the remaining pieces covered.

Flatten the dough slightly with a rolling pin, then thin it in a hand-crank pasta machine following the directions on page 11 or use a rolling pin following the directions on page 14. Do not make the dough too thin. If using a pasta machine, thin the dough to the next to the last setting.

Cut the dough using the vermicelli or fettucine cutter. The dough is very stretchy and resilient. Place the pici on clean kitchen towels or, to dry for long-term storage, hang the pici over dowel rods as described on page 16.

To cut by hand, follow the directions on page 14 and cut the pici either ⅛ or ¼ inch wide.

NOTE: *Both versions of pici can be made ahead, dried on dowel rods, and saved for future use. Pici will keep for months in a cool place loosely covered with aluminum foil.*

# Trenette

MAKES 1 POUND (SERVES 4 TO 6)

*Trenette (bavette) are thin noodles from Liguria made with water in addition to eggs and flour. I find that tap water can leave an aftertaste, so use filtered or bottled water if possible. The dough is very elastic and not as yellow as the basic recipe for Pasta Fatta a Mano (page 9).*

2½ cups unbleached all-purpose flour
½ cup semolina flour
1 teaspoon fine sea salt

2 large eggs
½ cup filtered water

Combine the flours and salt and mound on a work surface. With your fist, make a hole in the center of the mound. Break the eggs into the center and add the water. Mix with a fork to break up the yolks and blend in the water. Follow the directions on page 9 for mixing and kneading the dough and on page 14 for rolling, cutting, and drying the noodles. Cut trenette as for fettucine as described on page 11.

## TAGLIATELLE VERDI
# Green Tagliatelle

MAKES 1¼ POUNDS (SERVES 4 TO 6)

*Tagliatelle verdi are long strands of spinach-flavored homemade pasta typical of Emilia-Romagna. The Emilians also use this dough for lasagne, and I also use it to make fusilli (page 20). Spinach creates a wetter dough, so the most important thing to remember is to make sure that as much water as possible has been removed; too much remaining water and you will find yourself using much more flour than necessary. I prefer to make this pasta using a food processor because I can get a more even green color distribution of the spinach but I have also given a hand method for making it, which will not be as intense in color but more speckled-looking.*

One 10-ounce bag fresh spinach, stemmed and washed well

4 large eggs

½ cup durum semolina flour

2 teaspoons fine sea salt

2½ cups unbleached all-purpose flour

Place the spinach in a pot with no additional water. Cover and cook the spinach over medium heat just until the leaves are wilted. Drain the spinach in a colander and, when cool, squeeze out as much water as possible. You should have about ¾ cup of spinach.

Transfer the spinach to the bowl of a food processor, add the eggs, and process until the mixture is smooth. Add the semolina flour, salt, and 2 cups of the all-purpose flour and process into a coarse mixture. Remove the cover and feel the dough. If it is sticky, add the remaining flour 2 tablespoons at a time and process until a ball of dough is formed that leaves the sides of the bowl and is smooth and soft.

Remove the dough from the bowl of the processor and knead it on a lightly floured surface for 2 to 3 minutes. Allow the dough to rest for 30 minutes on a lightly floured surface under a bowl.

To make the dough by hand, mix the flours and salt together on a work surface with your hands and evenly blend the ingredients. Shape into a mound with a well in the center.

In a blender or food processor, puree the spinach. Set aside.

Crack the eggs into the center of the well. Add the spinach and combine the wet ingredients with a fork. In a clockwise fashion, begin bringing flour from the inside of the well into the egg mixture. When the mixture is thick and rough-looking, use your hands to incorporate enough remaining flour to make a smooth ball of dough. Push the excess flour aside, and work the dough on a lightly floured surface until smooth.

Cut the dough into four pieces. Work with one piece at a time and keep the rest covered. With a rolling pin, roll the dough out to a 9 × 5-inch rectangle. With a conventional hand-crank pasta machine, thin the dough using the settings on the machine as instructed on page 11. To roll the dough by hand, follow the instructions on page 14. The dough should not be so thin that it tears when lifted but rather you should be able to see the shadow of your hand when placed behind the strip of dough.

Drape the strips of dough over dowel rods following the directions on page 16. Allow the strips to dry just until they are no longer tacky, then use the fettucine setting to cut the strips or cut by hand ¼ inch wide. Drape the noodles over the dowel rods leaving space between each one. For long-term storage, allow the noodles to dry until they are very brittle and the ends have curled. Store the noodles in large sheets of aluminum foil loosely wrapped to keep from breaking the noodles. For immediate use, allow the noodles to dry about 15 minutes before cooking.

# Handmade Pappardelle

Pappardelle can vary in size from ¾ to 2 inches wide and 6 to 9 inches long. Use the basic dough for *Pasta Fatta a Mano* (see page 9). Divide the dough into four pieces and work with one piece at a time, keeping the rest covered.

On a lightly floured work surface, flatten each piece with a rolling pin. Thin the dough using the knob on the side of a hand-crank pasta machine to tighten the rollers. Thin the dough between ⅛ and ¼ inch thick. This usually means setting the knob to the highest number, which will vary depending on the type of machine. With a knife, trim the sheet to 36 inches long and 4 inches wide. Use a pastry wheel to cut 1- to 1½-inch-wide strips the length of the sheet of dough, then cut crosswise into 9-inch lengths for a total of sixteen strips. Or, if you have it, use the pappardelle attachment for a hand-crank pasta machine. Repeat the process for the remaining pieces of dough. Re-roll the scraps together and cut more pieces.

To roll the dough by hand, follow the instructions on page 14, then cut the pappardelle into strips as described above.

Lay the strips in single layers on clean kitchen towels and allow to dry for 30 minutes before cooking.

NOTE: *To make spinach pappardelle, use the recipe for Tagliatelle Verdi on page 20.*

# Tales of Tagliatelle, Truffles, and Trust

Sansepolcro, a reverent name meaning holy tomb, is an industrial town in eastern Tuscany, not too distant from Cortona, one of my favorite cities. Always reluctant to explore places in Italy that to me are too much in the realm of the "modern world," I was glad that I succumbed to Sansepolcro for two reasons: first, the great artist Piero della Francesca's masterpiece, *Resurrection*, depicting Christ rising from the tomb, is housed in the Museo Civico and stirs one's emotions with its timeless message of the triumph of good over evil, and, second, the most wonderful trattoria, Ristorante da Ventura on Via Aggunte, stirs one's appetite with lovingly prepared local cuisine where dining becomes an event in the family-owned restaurant of Gino Tofanelli, a jovial and gregarious fellow with a toothy smile who dispenses with offering cumbersome menus for hungry clients to peruse and instead makes the choice for you (with your permission, of course). Gino's clientele is mostly local and his wife is the chief cook, which to me are two good indications when looking for a restaurant in a strange place.

Sipping a glass of Brunello di Montalcino 1988 wine and munching on sawdust-dry breadsticks, which I hoped were not an indication of the quality of the food, I listened intently to what Gino was saying and reluctantly decided to leave my fate in his hands, since there were not that many restaurants from which to choose, which I reasoned was because Sansepolcro was not a must-see tourist destination.

Without hesitation, Gino's suggestion was to begin with a *primo piatto* (first course) of fresh tagliatelle with shaved white truffles, and his description of the dish was a long orchestration of his fondest feelings for local cooking. With tears in his eyes, he explained that the tagliatelle were made and cut by hand every day and the dough was rolled so thin by his wife that you could read a newspaper through it. The truffles were the freshest available, albeit for a hefty price, but, according to Gino, worth any price. As Gino prepared the dish tableside, he became like a maestro, shaving truffles with great fanfare. These almost see-through chips of woodsy flavor landed like delicate falling leaves on top of a steaming plate of buttery ribbons of almost translucent tagliatelle. The aroma of the truffles was hypnotic and they melted like butter in your mouth. The dish was pure and sim-

ple, the flavors a sublime balance of subtleness. Gino's eyes lit up when he saw my exuberant joy. Trust was definitely a virtue, no matter how bad the breadsticks were.

What dish could possibly follow to top this? I wanted to beg for seconds but knew that the culinary stage was set for the rest of the meal to follow and that it was best to adhere to tradition. Once the tagliatelle with shaved truffles was but a lasting memory, Gino, ever gregarious and flirty, tempted the taste buds once again with the house specials for the day, including roasted baby pork (*maiolino di porchetta*) with a crackling, bronze skin and the most delicious, moist-tasting meat; then came *stinco di vitello*, delicate and tender veal shank roasted very slowly in the oven and served with tiny rosemary-flavored potatoes (*patate al forno*) and creamy cannellini beans with roasted sweet red onions. Every dish was exquisite, and reminiscing about that meal in Sansepolcro really drove home that old adage "Never judge a book by its cover," to which I would also add: never judge an Italian restaurant by the quality of its breadsticks.

FARFALLONE DI DUE COLORI

# Large Two-Colored Butterflies

MAKES ABOUT 13 DOZEN

*Bow-tie pasta is a favorite of children and is better known in Italian as farfalle (butterflies). Farfallone are large butterflies and are fun to make from scratch, although there are very good commercially prepared brands on the market. In this recipe, two doughs are made, one plain, the other flavored with pureed beets, and the two doughs are thinned sandwiched together for two-color butterflies. Use the dough to make other sizes of farfalle. Dried farfalle can be stored in an airtight jar for several months. Use small butterflies (farfalline) in soup, serve farfalle or farfallone in a creamy besciamella sauce (page 48), or make an easy timballo (page 145).*

**FOR THE PLAIN PASTA**
*(makes 12 ounces)*

2 extra large eggs

⅛ teaspoon fine sea salt

1½ cups unbleached all-purpose flour

6 tablespoons finely ground durum flour

**FOR THE BEET PASTA**
*(makes 12 ounces)*

2 extra large eggs

⅛ teaspoon fine sea salt

2½ tablespoons pureed cooked beets (about 1 small) (see Note)

2 to 2½ cups unbleached all-purpose flour

For making the plain pasta by hand, follow the directions for Pasta Fatta a Mano (page 9). Knead the dough until it is smooth and no longer sticky. Place it under a bowl on a lightly floured surface and let it rest for 30 minutes.

To make the dough in a food processor, follow the directions on page 10.

To make the beet pasta, follow the directions for *Pasta Fatta a Mano* (page 9) or for making the dough in a food processor (page 10), adding the pureed beets with the eggs.

Divide each dough into four balls. Work with one piece of each color at a time; keep the rest covered. Flatten each piece of dough with a rolling pin. Thin the plain dough using a pasta machine set to the thinnest setting. Trim the sheet to 22 inches square. Likewise thin the beet dough and trim it to 22 inches square.

Place the sheet of beet dough on top of the plain dough and press down slightly with your hands to adhere the two together. Roll the dough on the thinnest setting to 32 inches. Cut the sheet crosswise in half to make two 16-inch-long sheets. Cut each half in half again lengthwise with a pastry wheel to form two strips. Cut eight 2-inch squares from each strip. Re-roll the scraps to form more farfallone.

Pinch each piece together in the center with your fingers to form the butterfly or bow-tie shape, then twist one side of the bow tie under from the center so one half is plain-colored and the other is red. Place on a clean kitchen towel. Repeat with the remaining

*continued*

dough. Let the farfalle dry for 30 minutes before cooking or let them dry completely for several days and store in airtight containers.

## Variation

Tomato paste or pureed spinach or cooked and pureed carrots can be used in place of the beets.

TIP: Place the thinned sandwiched sheet of dough over a 12- or 24-compartment ravioli form and roll over the dough with a rolling pin. Form into farfalle as described above.

NOTE: *To cook the beets, cut the stem off one small beet, leaving about 2 inches of it still attached. Wrap the beet in aluminum foil and bake in a preheated 350°F oven until soft, about 25 to 30 minutes. Alternately, cook the beet in boiling water to cover or in the microwave. When cool enough to handle, peel away the skin and puree in a food processor or blender.*

## Making two-colored butterflies

*Evenly trimming the two strips of dough.*

*Placing the beet strip on top of the plain strip of dough.*

*Thinning the two strips together through the pasta machine.*

*Cutting the thinned dough strip into 2-inch squares.*

*Pinching the center of the square together to form the butterfly.*

*Twisting the farfallone (butterflies).*

*Farfallone di Due Colori
(page 23) served with Salsa
di Besciamella (page 48)*

## FUSILLI CASALINGHI

# Homemade Fusilli

MAKES AT LEAST 22 DOZEN

*In Pino Correnti's work* Il Libro d'Oro della Cucina e Dei Vini di Sicilia, *there is a wonderful description of the ingenious method that Sicilian fishermen used to shape a coiled pasta called fusilli. They simply used thin fishing rods* (canna da pesca) *to entwine and shape them, leaving them to dry in the sizzling Sicilian sun. If you want to try making them, round metal barbecue skewers work well for achieving the characteristic shape. Without a doubt this is time-consuming work, and best done when you have extra help around, but I have made them* da sola *(by myself) and in an hour had a mound of little coils. Fusilli are just plain fun to make and eat and children love them for their chewiness and charming look. For me it brings back many fond memories of eating these slippery squiggles with a big towel wrapped around my neck and with soup spoon in hand, scooting around the bowl, trying to conquer them. There are many good brands of commercially prepared fusilli, and I often use them, but sometimes I like to make them using the basic pasta recipe on page 9 or the recipe on page 20 for Tagliatelle Verdi (spinach-flavored pasta). The Salsa di Pomodori Mozzarella ed Acciughe on page 53 pairs wonderfully with the plain fusilli; pair the spinach-flavored fusilli with the Salsa di Besciamella on page 48.*

1 recipe Handmade Pasta dough (page 9)

Cut the dough into four pieces and work with one piece at a time, keeping the remaining pieces covered.

Use a rolling pin to flatten the dough, then thin it following the directions on page 11 using a hand-crank pasta machine or a rolling pin until it is ⅛ inch thick.

Trim the dough to 27 inches long by 4½ inches wide. Cut six 4½-inch squares from the dough, then cut the squares as for fettucine, using the cutter on a hand-crank pasta machine, or use a knife and cut ¼-inch-wide strips.

Place the end of a strip of dough over an 8-inch-long metal skewer and wrap the pasta loosely around the skewer, leaving slightly open spaces as you wrap the dough. (Another method is to simply pinch off pieces of dough the size of large peas, roll them under your hand until they are 6 to 7 inches long, and then wrap them around the skewer.) Lay the skewers on a clean kitchen towel and allow to set for about 5 to 10 minutes. Then slide the fusilli off the skewers and transfer them to clean towels. Let them rest 20 minutes before cooking or dry them thoroughly for long storage; this may take up to 2 days.

NOTE: *Fusilli can be shaped into longer lengths by pinching off larger pieces of dough.*

# Making fusilli

Pinching pieces the size of large peas off the ball of dough.

Rolling each piece into a long rope.

Wrapping the dough around a skewer.

Sliding the partially dried fusilli off the skewer.

# Garganelli

MAKES AT LEAST 6 DOZEN (SERVES 8 TO 10)

*Garganelli, which means "small esophagus," is a pasta from Emilia-Romagna that is difficult to find outside of that region. Admittedly, it takes a bit of time and patience to hand-form the pointed tubular shape that resembles penne, but they are so delicious that I encourage you to try them. The nutmeg-and-Parmesan-cheese-flavored dough is easily made in a food processor and is smooth and elastic. Allowing the dough to rest, covered, for about 1 hour, makes it easy to roll either in a pasta machine or by hand.*

3 large eggs

2 tablespoons freshly grated Parmigiano-Reggiano cheese

⅛ teaspoon freshly grated nutmeg

2¼ cups unbleached all-purpose flour

Whirl the eggs, cheese, and nutmeg together in a food processor until smooth. Gradually add the flour until a ball of dough is formed that leaves the sides of the bowl. Gather up the dough, shape it into a ball, and let it rest, covered, under a bowl for about 1 hour.

Alternately, make the dough by hand. Heap the flour onto a work surface and fashion it into a *fontana* (page 8). Crack the eggs into the center of the *fontana* and break them up with a fork. Beat in the cheese and nutmeg. Form the dough following the technique on page 9.

When ready to roll and form the garganelli, cut the dough into four pieces; work with one piece at a time, keeping the rest covered. Roll out each piece following the directions on page 11, using a hand-crank pasta machine or by hand using a rolling pin. Trim the sheet to 24 inches long. The sheet should be about 6 inches wide. With a pasta wheel, cut the sheet in half lengthwise, then cut eight 3-inch squares from each half. There should be sixteen 3-inch squares. Save and re-roll the scraps. Repeat with the remaining dough.

Place a new unsharpened pencil or small ¼-inch-wide wooden dowel rod diagonally at a point at one end of the pasta and roll the pasta up on the pencil or dowel rod. Create lines on the garganelli by rolling the pasta over a new clean comb, a butter paddle, or a *chitarra* (page 6). Slip the garganelli off the end of the pencil or rod and let them dry on clean kitchen towels for about 30 minutes before cooking.

NOTE: *Garganelli are best cooked the day they are made. Drying them for future use makes them too hard to cook uniformly.*

## How to Cook Pasta

I don't know how many times someone has asked me this question: "Why does my pasta stick together when I cook it and why is it so gummy-tasting?" Cooking pasta correctly eludes many people, so here are some helpful tips for cooking both dried pasta (*pasta secca*) and fresh pasta (*pasta fresca*) that can help ensure that your pasta cooks properly each time.

### DRIED PASTA (*Pasta Secca*)

The success of any commercially prepared dried pasta is determined first of all by the type of flour used to make it. Pasta imported from Italy is made from 100 percent semolina flour, a hard wheat flour with a high protein content. Before you buy, make sure the words "Made with 100 percent durum semolina flour" appear on the label, and do not buy dried pasta made from "enriched flour," which tends to be a softer flour with not enough gluten to give pasta the structure it needs to hold up in cooking and not become mushy.

Water is another consideration. Many of Italy's largest commercial pasta companies, like Barilla, Del Verde, De Cecco, and Molisana, tout the fact that they use the purest mountain spring water to make pasta, and it is true that quality water does not impart an aftertaste. If you have poor quality water you may want to use bottled still water.

Buying the right kind of pasta is the first step. The next step is the pot in which you cook the pasta. I would not be without a 7- to 8-quart-capacity pasta pot with a colander insert that allows for easy lifting from the cooking water and draining of the pasta (see mail-order sources, page 160). When you are ready to cook the pasta, fill the pot with the insert with 4 to 6 quarts of water for every pound of pasta. If you have

filtered tap water, use it. Bring the water to a rolling boil, salt it using 1 tablespoon per 4 quarts of water, then add the pasta.

The reason so many people fail to cook pasta correctly is due to not using enough water to allow for the pasta to expand during the cooking process. Some cooks think that adding oil to the cooking water will eliminate this problem, but it only compounds it and I have never seen this practice in Italy. Adding oil will leave a slimy coating on pasta and make it very difficult for sauce to adhere to it.

If you are cooking spaghetti or other long types of pasta, fan the spaghetti out with your hands before putting it into the water. Use a wooden spoon or spaghetti fork to submerge the pasta below the waterline. Stir once, place the lid on the pot, and bring the water to a boil, then uncover and cook the pasta until it is *al dente,* that is, it is firm, keeps its shape, does not collapse or look soggy, and yet is cooked when you bite into it. If you are cooking short cuts of pasta like rigatoni or fusilli, add them all at once to the water, stir with a wooden spoon, cover, bring to a boil, then remove the cover and stir once again.

Frozen filled pasta is another matter. Adding, for example, frozen ravioli to the boiling water will bring down the temperature of the water and it will take longer for the water to come back to the boil. In this case, cook the ravioli or other filled pasta in small batches, removing them with a skimmer or pasta scoop as they are cooked and transferring them to a heated bowl or platter. Keep them warm and covered until all the cooking is complete.

Knowing when pasta is sufficiently cooked is learned only by trial and error. In Italy, pasta is cooked much firmer than it is here, and remember that pasta continues to cook a bit more even when it is drained. Sample the pasta as it is cooking to determine when it is done. Thicker pasta like orecchiette (little ears) or farfalle (butterflies) will take longer to cook uniformly. Instructions on store-bought packages give a range of 10 to 20 minutes, depending on the cut, but often-times this is too long and results in soggy pasta. For casserole-type dishes requiring boiling the pasta and then baking it, it is best to undercook the pasta just a bit since it will cook again in the oven.

As soon as the pasta is cooked, drain it by lifting the insert out of the pot and shake off the excess water but allow a little to remain since this will help to evenly distribute the sauce (see also the classic *ripassatura* method for mixing pasta, water, and sauce). Pour the pasta from the insert onto a large shallow platter or into a shallow bowl. Add the desired sauce and toss to mix well.

To drain unfilled pasta using a large pot with no insert, place a colander in the sink. Bring the pot from the stove top and drain the pasta into the colander.

### FRESH PASTA (*Pasta Fresca*)

Cooking fresh pasta is a much quicker process than cooking dried pasta. Since it is fresh, it will cook in less than 3 minutes if it is a cut like fettucine, spaghetti, or vermicelli. Fresh sheets of lasagne noodles will also cook very quickly, as will stuffed pasta such as ravioli and cappelletti.

Follow the procedure above for removing fresh unfilled pasta, but for filled pasta, use a pasta scoop or a slotted spoon to gently remove the pasta in batches from the water. To try to drain filled pasta by empty-ing it from the pot all at once into a colander is to court disaster, as dropping delicate filled types will cause breakage and fillings to leak out.

Whichever type of pasta you are cooking, remember that once it is sauced, it should be served immediately.

## The Ripassatura

I wish I had a nickel for every time someone told me about the correct way to mix cooked pasta and sauce. Some Italian cooks will shake their heads and emphat-ically assert that the pasta must be thoroughly drained before being combined with the sauce. Others will denounce this practice as heresy and declare that pasta must not be drained too well or the sauce will not blend with it. The latter group are advocates of a prac-tice known as the *ripassatura,* meaning, to return to the pot, which involves saving a little of the pasta cooking water, then returning it with the pasta to the cooking pot and adding the prepared sauce, then stir-ring it quickly over low heat to smooth it out to pro-vide just the right, evenly distributed film of flavor necessary to lightly coat the pasta. It is important that this action take but a few minutes, no more, or the pasta could become overcooked.

This method is especially good for commercially prepared *pasta secca* (dried pasta) and thicker types of sauce, but I do not recommend it for delicate filled-type pasta such as ravioli where the quick stirring action could cause the pasta to tear and lose its filling.

The one thing all Italian cooks do agree upon is that pasta should never be hidden under a dense cover of sauce that sits in a clump directly in the middle of the serving dish. So the next time you cook pasta, practice the *ripassatura* and decide for yourself.

## Pass the Parmigiano-Reggiano— and Other Italian Cheeses

It is a daily ritual played out at the dinner table . . . steaming plates of pasta blanketed in thick tomato sauce and sprinkled with "Parmesan cheese" from a box.

A scene like this would be unthinkable in Italy because Italians take the quality and authenticity of their cheeses as seriously as they do their pasta. And just as there are hundreds of regional pastas, there are an equal number of regional cheeses, both aged and fresh.

Outside of Italy, the two most widely known aged cheeses used for grating are Parmesan (Parmigiano-Reggiano) and Pecorino and the most popular fresh cheese is ricotta. Parmigiano-Reggiano is a cow's milk cheese, while Pecorino is a sheep's milk cheese, and ricotta is a fresh cheese made from whey, the leftovers of the cheese-making process. While these cheeses are found in all the regions of Italy, Parmigiano-Reggiano has traditionally been recognized as the cheese that northern Italians use and Pecorino the preferred cheese of southern Italians.

We tend to think of Parmigiano-Reggiano and Pecorino as cheese *only* used for grating, sprinkled on top of pasta dishes, but in Italy chips of these cheeses are whittled out of a wedge with a tiny cheese knife and eaten on their own, sometimes with a dribble of balsamic vinegar, as is the case with Parmigiano-Reggiano. Pecorino cheese has been the familiar lunch of shepherds in Italy for centuries; a popular snack is pieces of Pecorino eaten with fresh fava beans, some coarse bread, and a glass of wine.

Unfortunately, many people resort to purchasing what they think are these cheeses, conveniently grated and sold in shaker-type containers. But they are often no more than artificial imitations, bearing no resemblance to the real thing. Real Parmigiano-Reggiano and Pecorino cheese are available in most supermarkets and in Italian specialty stores and, if not, can be mail-ordered (page 160).

True, it is difficult to find some types of Italian cheeses but availability is improving as supermarkets and specialty cheese stores expand their inventory. It is also true that the best place to enjoy many of these cheeses, especially the delicate soft and fresh types, is in Italy, in the locales where they are made. But realism must rule in the kitchen and we must learn to choose wisely and use Italian products that are available here.

Get to know these cheeses by looking for their names embedded on their rinds. The production of Parmigiano-Reggiano is controlled by law and no cheese is released for sale until it meets all requirements. When it does, the stamp of approval of the Consorzio del Formaggio Parmigiano-Reggiano is branded on the cheese rind, indicating that this is the real thing.

Never buy Parmigiano-Reggiano or Pecorino cheese already grated; there is no way of telling if these are, in fact, the real products of Italy and could be imitations from elsewhere. A good indicator is the price; if it is inexpensive, it probably is not the real thing. Parmigiano-Reggiano is expensive, even in Italy, but a little goes a long way. Purchase a wedge that will be used within a short period of time. It is better to buy it frequently than to let the cheese languish, insufficiently wrapped, in the refrigerator, where it will dry out and be impossible to grate. After purchasing the cheese, wrap it first in damp cheesecloth, then tightly in plastic wrap, and finally seal the piece in aluminum foil and refrigerate it. Bring the cheese to room temperature before eating or grating it.

The list that follows provides a brief description of the most readily available Italian cheeses; many of them are used in the recipes in this book.

*Asiago:* Cow's milk cheese produced in northern Italy (Vicenza, Padova, and Treviso). When young it has a mild, nutty flavor; as it ages the flavor is more pronounced. A good grating cheese that also melts well and is a favorite addition to cream sauces.

**Fior di latte:** Snowy white balls of fresh, soft cow's milk mozzarella cheese produced in Abruzzi-Molise and Campania. The smaller balls are called *bocconcini*.

**Fontina:** Soft, high-fat cow's milk cheese produced in the Val d'Aosta. It has a creamy, mild taste and is wonderful as a melting cheese for fillings or for sauces for pasta. Italian Fontina is recognized by its brown rind.

**Gorgonzola:** Cow's milk cheese produced in Lombardia and injected with penicillin mold, which gives the cheese its characteristic blue veining.

**Mozzarella:** A hand-stretched fresh cheese made from buffalo milk in Campania. It is delicate in texture and very mild and creamy in taste. This cheese is very perishable and, when available, very costly. Substitute fresh cow's milk mozzarella (*fior di latte*), which is more readily available and less expensive, but don't expect the flavor to be the same.

**Parmigiano-Reggiano:** Referred to as the king of Italian cheeses, this large round cheese, weighing between 48 and 85 pounds, is made of part-skim cow's milk. Its production is controlled by law and it can only be made in the provinces of Parma, Mantua, Reggio Emilia, Modena, and Bologna. The rind is stamped repeatedly with the words Parmigiano-Reggiano to ensure authenticity. The finely grained cheese is straw-yellow in color with white specks of whey. The cheese ages anywhere from 18 to 24 months, and is still being made today in accordance with methods dating to the eleventh century. In Italy, this is an eating cheese as well as a grating cheese.

**Pecorino:** A sheep's milk cheese whose origins go back to antiquity. This is still the cheese of shepherds in parts of Italy, especially Sicily, Sardinia, and Lazio. Aging varies for this cheese that is slightly salty and is sometimes made with black or green peppercorns. The name after the word Pecorino indicates where it is made: Pecorino Romano from around Rome, Pecorino Sardo from Sardinia, and so on.

**Provolone:** A full-fat cow's milk cheese from southern Italy. Aged, it is a good cheese for grating.

**Ricotta:** Soft, fresh cheese made from the whey left over from the cheese-making process; it can be sheep's milk or cow's milk. A dried, salted version suitable for grating is called ricotta salata.

**Taleggio:** Soft, high-fat cow's milk cheese from Lombardia, it has a reddish-brown rind and a very rich taste. A wonderful table cheese as well as a melting cheese for use in fillings and cream sauces.

# Pasta in Soup

BRODO DI PASTINA E POLPETTINE

# Pastina in Broth with Tiny Meatballs

SERVES 4

*Chicken broth and pastina, that was the soup that nourished me when I was a sick child, and the tradition continued with my children. Surely, tiny specks of pasta floating in a clear broth could stymie the most stubborn cold and when it vanished the request was still there for pastina in other guises as well; cooked and mixed with lots of butter and grated Parmigiano-Reggiano cheese, or with tomato sauce. Another favorite soup was pastina with marble-size meatballs, often served as a first course to Sunday dinner. Baking the meatballs instead of frying them keeps them light and tender, and eliminates adding any additional fat. Having chicken broth on hand makes this a soup that can be ready in no time.*

¼ cup fresh bread crumbs

2 tablespoons milk

¼ pound ground beef chuck

2 teaspoons freshly grated Pecorino cheese

1 teaspoon grated lemon zest

¼ teaspoon fine sea salt

1 scant teaspoon ground cloves

2 quarts homemade (page 35) or canned low-sodium chicken broth

½ cup pastina or other small soup pasta such as stelline or orzo

Combine the bread crumbs and milk in a small bowl and set aside. In a medium-size bowl, mix the chuck, cheese, lemon zest, salt, and cloves just enough to combine the ingredients. Gently mix in the bread-crumb-and-milk mixture.

Preheat the oven to 350°F.

Form tiny meatballs using about ½ teaspoon of the mixture and roll each ball between the palms of your hands. To keep your hands from sticking, dip them in water occasionally.

Place the meatballs in an 8-inch baking pan or dish; bake them for 6 to 8 minutes, then remove them from the pan with a slotted spoon and place them on a paper-towel-lined dish to drain.

Meanwhile, bring the chicken broth to a boil in a pot. Stir in the pastina and cook until *al dente*, 10 to 12 minutes. Stir in the meatballs, lower the heat to medium, and cook about 3 minutes longer. Serve immediately with additional grated cheese if desired.

NOTE: *The meatballs can be made and frozen after cooking for future use. They'll keep for several months. Other broths, such as beef, veal, and vegetable, can also be used.*

BRODO DI POLLO

# Homemade Chicken Broth

MAKES 3½ TO 4 QUARTS

*It is always a good idea to keep homemade broths on hand; they are easy to make ahead and can be frozen for future use. If canned broths are used, be sure that they are the low-salt varieties, as regular canned broth can be very salty, and even the low-sodium ones are a bit too salty for my liking. Chilling homemade broth overnight allows the fat to collect on the surface where you can easily skim it away, leaving a clear and light-tasting broth.*

4 pounds chicken parts (necks, wings, and breast bones)

2 teaspoons coarse sea salt

2 cloves garlic, cut in half

2 large onions, peeled and quartered

2 fresh or canned plum tomatoes quartered

1 bay leaf

2 sprigs each fresh Italian parsley and basil, tied together with kitchen string

Juice of 1 lemon

2 ribs celery with leaves, cut into 4 pieces

2 carrots, peeled and halved

5 black peppercorns, crushed

Put the chicken pieces in a large stockpot, then add the salt and enough cold water to cover the pieces. Cover the pot and bring to a boil. Skim off the foam that collects with a spoon. Add the remaining ingredients, reduce the heat to medium-low, and simmer, covered, for 45 minutes to 1 hour. Skim off any additional foam that collects as the broth cooks.

Remove the chicken pieces with a slotted spoon and reserve for another use. Pour the broth and vegetables into a large strainer lined with damp cheesecloth set over another pot. With the back of a spoon, press on the vegetables to release all the juices. Discard the solids left in the strainer. Let cool, then cover the broth with plastic wrap and refrigerate overnight.

With a spoon, remove the congealed fat from the top of the broth. The broth is ready to use. It can be refrigerated for up to 1 week or frozen for up to 3 months.

# La Cenone in Polverara

## *The Big Dinner in Polverara*

How dare we invite Italians to dinner in their own home! My husband, Guy, and I and our friends Bert and Betty were houseguests of our friend Luciano Berti, who lives in Florence but has a summer home in Polverara, a tiny hamlet about an hour and a half's drive from Florence. To show our appreciation for his hospitality, we decided to prepare dinner for Luciano and his girlfriend, Barbara. As we discussed the idea with Luciano, I discovered that his parents, Emma and Franco, lived next door on weekends and so it seemed fitting to ask them to come, too. Now the number of guests began to snowball because Luciano also asked several other friends and his parents were going to bring along two of their friends as well. We were now cooking for thirteen people.

We planned a grocery shopping adventure for early the next day to the nearby town of Sasso Marconi. This had to be right. We shopped for prosciutto and melon, for good bread, figs, and pork sausage. The pastry shops in Sasso Marconi did not tempt me, so I decided to make

something American, a fruit cobbler. I had noticed the plum trees around Luciano's house and decided that fresh plucked plums would do nicely for my cobbler. I would pick them when we returned.

The first course was going to be supplied by Franco, homemade *tortellini in brodo.* How could we say no? That off our minds, we began the preparations for the rest of the meal. Crowding in the tiny kitchen with bags of groceries, we assigned tasks. I got to work making the cobbler, Guy cleaned the salad greens, Betty chopped peppers and garlic to go with the pork sausage, and Bert cleaned and snipped green beans and picked mint to make our marinated salad. We had asked everyone to come at 8:30 P.M., a respectable gathering hour before dinner in Italian homes. I retreated with basket in hand to pick plums. Luciano's Uncle Beppi was strolling by and as I searched for just the right ones we engaged in conversation about the land and the fruit trees. As he helped me pick the plums, he talked of the little hamlet of Polverara and the house where Luciano lived as once being a part of a monastery. I thanked him for his help and started toward the house when I heard a car come roaring up the dirt driveway leaving a storm of dust clouds in its wake. Emma and Franco were arriving for the weekend

from the city. I waved and they stopped the car. They were both very excited as they got out of the car and motioned me to come toward the trunk. Their precious cargo took up the entire trunk space, a large wooden crate spilling over with hundreds of plump and dazzling yellow tortellini, our *primo piatto* (first course) for dinner. I could hardly contain my joy and looked forward to this wonderful classic dish.

Franco said he would be over shortly but first he needed to get the broth for the tortellini from his kitchen and asked if I would like to come and see his wine cellar as well. I told him as soon as I finished the plum cobbler, I would come over.

Franco had wines from World War II in his cellar and proceeded to tell me about them. I felt privileged to be in this dusty, cobwebbed cantina listening to Franco retell stories of long ago. Upstairs Emma was making *crostini,* small toasts topped with tomatoes and *mostarda di frutta,* a candied fruit concoction that is traditionally used with *bollito misto* (boiled meats). She also showed me her method of making quick tomato sauce. Emma is from Naples and keeps close to her roots in the kitchen. Looking at my watch, I knew I needed to get back to the kitchen and as I said my good-byes, she asked me about the *antipasti* I had prepared: *melone con prosciutto,* I said, feeling now that this was inadequate.

Franco followed with the capon broth for the tortellini. We were nearly ready; the table looked lovely with the new linen cloth I had purchased for Luciano and the flower arrangement lent a welcoming air. It seemed strange to be welcoming Luciano and his friends and family to his own home.

Finally, everyone arrived and introductions were made. Barbara worked at the British Institute; Rachel and Rosalie at Gucci's, and Iris and Joni, Franco's and Emma's friends, lived in Florence and were into music. We all enjoyed small talk while sampling the *antipasti.* Finally, with great fanfare, Franco announced that the moment for cooking the tortellini had arrived. The broth was boiling, rumbling in a huge pot and, without hesitation, Franco dumped the entire crateful of tortellini into the pot and that is when the evening meal took control of us. Before we knew what was happening the broth boiled over the rim of the pot onto the stove top and down its sides onto the floor, which caused an electrical outage in the process. We stood silent in total darkness. *"Ma che successo?"* ("What happened?") Franco moaned. Luciano quickly hurried downstairs to see if he could reengage the fuse

box, but no luck. Out came the candles, which I felt set a very nice mood for our dinner, but I wondered how the rest of the meal would get done with no power. The men went in unison to the fuse box again, this time with success. After all the commotion, we finally returned to our melon and prosciutto. It was delicious, the melon perfumed and sweet, the prosciutto delicate pink in color and mild in flavor, a safe choice, I thought to myself.

Then Franco served the remains of the soup, still moaning about the disaster. The first mouthful encapsulated all that is wonderful about this classic dish from Emilia-Romagna: clear and tasty broth, delicate egg pasta, and a filling of three meats with Parmigiano-Reggiano cheese. I secretly hoped that the rest of the meal would measure up.

The *secondo* of *salsicce fresche con peperoni* (fresh sausage with peppers) was enjoyed by all, and Luciano was so pleased that we took advantage of the wild mint growing near the house for the bean salad. We drank Franco's wine and I mentally took note of the whole dinner scene, which now had lasted for hours; how wonderful, I thought, how the power of simply prepared food could bind people together, whether they were friends or strangers.

The plum cobbler was a hit, especially when I announced that the plums were from their very own trees. Emma wanted the "recipe." Now satiated and the hour growing very late, Luciano brought out nocino, a green walnut liqueur made yearly on the feast of St. John, on June 24. Mahogany-colored when aged, it is very powerful and I sipped it gingerly, knowing that a stack of dirty dishes awaited my attention after everyone left.

Kisses on both cheeks for everyone and an admonition from Franco that we should *dormite bene* (sleep well) ended our evening. We all agreed that it had gone well and laughed about the power outage as we viewed a stove top now encrusted with dried broth, a few stray tortellini stuck in the stove top grates, and a mountain of dirty dishes and glassware piled on the table.

Tomorrow was another day, but tonight we had made the world seem smaller.

## CAPPELLETTI IN BRODO DI CAPONE

# Little Hats in Capon Broth

MAKES 150 TO 200

*"Cappelletti in brodo" were some of the first Italian words I learned from my Nonna Galasso. It was she who taught my mother and me how to make the little stuffed pasta hats that we ate on holidays and for special occasions. Needless to say, it was a ritual to make them and the time expended forming and filling them provided the forum for many folksy stories about my grandmother's life growing up in Belizzi in the province of Avellino. She never compromised on the filling ingredients, insisting that three meats—veal, pork, and beef—were necessary for a good filling and that the broth had to be homemade from the finest capon one could buy. The broth can be made several days ahead or frozen. The filling can be made 2 days ahead. To make and freeze the cappelletti, follow the instructions below. To use only partial amounts of this recipe calculate 2 cups of broth per eight cappelletti.*

2 tablespoons extra virgin olive oil

1 center-cut boneless pork chop (¼ pound), trimmed of fat and cubed

¼ pound boneless sirloin steak, cubed

¼ pound boneless veal chop, cubed

1 large egg

⅓ cup freshly grated Parmigiano-Reggiano cheese

2 tablespoons minced fresh Italian parsley leaves

1 tablespoon grated lemon zest

¼ teaspoon freshly grated nutmeg

¾ teaspoon fine sea salt

Freshly ground black pepper to taste

1 recipe Handmade Pasta dough (page 9)

1 recipe Capon Broth (recipe follows)

Heat the olive oil over medium heat in a medium-size sauté pan, then brown all the meat cubes evenly. Remove them from the pan to a dish and let cool.

In a meat grinder or a food processor, grind the meats very fine and transfer them to a bowl. Add the egg, cheese, parsley, zest, nutmeg, salt, and pepper and mix well. Cover and refrigerate until ready to use.

Divide the pasta dough into four pieces. Work with one piece at a time and keep the remaining pieces cov-

ered so they don't dry out. Flatten the dough slightly with a rolling pin and thin the pieces in a pasta machine following the directions on page 11 until the dough is about 1⁄16 inch thick. Do not make the dough so thin that the filling will break through it. Alternately, roll each piece of dough by hand with a rolling pin on a floured surface following the directions on page 14.

Use a 1-inch round cookie cutter or small glass to cut out rounds from each sheet of dough. (Re-roll the scraps and cut out more circles.) Place about ½ teaspoon of the filling in the center of each round. Fold each round in half to create a half-moon shape and pinch the edges closed; moisten the edges with water if necessary. Take the two pointed ends and bring them together to meet; pinch to seal them, creating the little hat. Place the cappelletti in single layers on clean kitchen towels or baking sheets lined with towels.

To prepare ten servings, bring the capon broth to a boil, add seven dozen of the cappelletti and cook them until they bob to the surface. Serve in the broth with extra grated Parmigiano-Reggiano cheese if desired.

TIP: Chill the filling and form pea-size balls ahead, then simply place in the center of cut-out circles of dough; this eliminates having to measure and place the filling on the circles each time and keeps your hands clean.

TIP: To freeze cappelletti, arrange them in single rows on a baking sheet. Cover the sheet loosely with aluminum foil and place the sheet in the freezer. When the cappelletti are hard, transfer them to airtight plastic bags and freeze them for up to 4 months. Add them frozen to boiling broth. They may take a few minutes longer to cook.

## BRODO DI CAPONE

# Capon Broth

MAKES ABOUT 5 QUARTS

One 4-pound capon, washed and cut into pieces

2½ teaspoons coarse salt

1 large clove garlic, peeled

2 medium-size onions, peeled and quartered

1 pound fresh or canned plum tomatoes, peeled, seeded, and coarsely chopped

2 sprigs fresh Italian parsley

2 sprigs fresh basil

2 sprigs fresh thyme

1 bay leaf

Juice of 1 lemon

2 ribs celery, cut into quarters

2 large carrots, peeled and cut into quarters

6 black peppercorns

Place the capon pieces in a 7- or 8-quart stockpot, then add the salt and cold water to cover the pieces. Cover the pot and bring the water to a boil. Uncover the pot and skim the foam that collects at the top with a skimmer. Add the garlic, onions, and tomatoes and stir well. Reduce the heat to medium-low. Tie the parsley, basil, and thyme together with kitchen string and add it to the pot. Add the remaining ingredients and simmer, covered, until the capon pieces are tender, 45 minutes to 1 hour.

Remove the capon pieces with a slotted spoon and reserve the meat for another use. Pour the soup and vegetables through a large strainer lined with cheesecloth into another pot or large bowl. Press on the solids with the back of a wooden spoon to extract all their juices. Discard the solids left in the strainer.

Cover the soup and refrigerate overnight. With a spoon, remove the congealed fat from the surface of the soup. The broth is ready to use or can be frozen for up to 3 months.

ZUPPA DI ALFABETO

# Alphabet Soup

MAKES ABOUT 2 QUARTS

*Who does not recall spelling out his or her name in steaming bowls of alphabet soup as a child? For me it is an enduring memory of good comfort food from home. In this simple but very tasty soup, tiny alphabet pasta is cooked in boiling homemade vegetable broth, which can be made ahead and frozen so it is always on hand. The secret to the flavor of this soup is the long cooking time.*

| | |
|---|---|
| 2 onions, peeled and quartered | 4 sprigs fresh thyme |
| 2 leeks, bulb part only, cut into quarters | 1 bay leaf |
| 2 large carrots, peeled and cut into chunks | 1 teaspoon black peppercorns, crushed |
| 2 potatoes, peeled and quartered | 4 or 5 cloves |
| 3 ribs celery, cut into chunks | Fine sea salt to taste |
| 5 ripe plum tomatoes, cut into chunks | 2 tablespoons fresh lemon juice |
| 1 large clove garlic, peeled | 8 cups water |
| 1 small bunch fresh Italian parsley | 1 cup alphabet macaroni |

Put all the ingredients except the macaroni in a large stockpot and bring to a boil over high heat. Reduce the heat to medium-low and simmer, covered, for 2 hours.

Place a large colander lined with damp cheesecloth over a large bowl. Strain the broth through the colander, pressing on the vegetables with the back of a wooden spoon to release all the juices. Discard the solids in the colander.

Return the soup to a soup pot and bring to a boil. Add the macaroni and cook until the pasta is *al dente*. Ladle the soup into bowls and serve immediately.

NOTE: *Cubes of fresh mozzarella cheese are delicious stirred into the soup just before serving.*

ZUPPA DI PASTA E CECE

# Pasta and Chickpea Soup

MAKES 2½ QUARTS

*Pasta and cece (chickpea) is a classic soup dish with many variations, as is this one. This is the kind of nourishing soup that falls into the category of a "meal in a pot," because it has a little bit of everything, from bits of Italian bacon (pancetta) to tomatoes, chickpeas, leeks, and pasta, and is very satisfying with homemade bread, a green salad, and fruit for a complete supper. I prefer to use dried chickpeas that I soak overnight; if you use canned chickpeas, be sure to rinse them well to rid them of the sodium. This soup tastes even better when made ahead.*

1 cup dried chickpeas, picked over (or rinsed and drained canned chickpeas to equal 2½ cups)

2½ cups cold water

1 cup small soup pasta such as anelletti or ditalini

4 cups boiling salted water

1 tablespoon extra virgin olive oil

¼ pound pancetta or bacon, diced

1 pound leeks (white and light green parts), washed well and thinly sliced

1 teaspoon dried red pepper flakes

4 cups canned crushed tomatoes

4 cups Homemade Chicken Broth (page 35) or canned low-sodium broth or water

¼ teaspoon freshly ground black pepper

1½ teaspoons fine sea salt

2 tablespoons Pesto Sauce (page 64)

1 tablespoon minced fresh rosemary leaves

Put the dried chickpeas in a bowl, cover them with water, and let soak overnight. The next day drain the chickpeas, place them in a soup pot with the 2½ cups of water. Bring to a boil and cook the chickpeas for 5 minutes. Drain and set aside. If using canned chickpeas, rinse, drain, and set aside

In another pot, cook the pasta in the boiling salted water until *al dente*. Drain the pasta, transfer to a bowl, and set aside.

In the same soup pot used to cook the chickpeas, heat the olive oil, then add the pancetta and leeks and cook over medium heat until the pancetta starts to brown and the leeks are soft. Add the red pepper flakes, tomatoes, chicken broth or water, black pepper, salt, and the chickpeas. Bring the mixture to a boil and cook, covered, over medium-high heat until the chickpeas are still firm but tender, 12 to 15 minutes. Stir in the pasta, pesto, and rosemary and serve immediately.

NOTE: *The rinds of Parmigiano-Reggiano cheese add wonderful taste when cooked in the soup (see Tip, page 45). Add them along with the chicken broth or water.*

NOTE: *Freeze the soup in plastic containers for future quick meals.*

*Zuppa di Tre Zucche con Orzo (Three-Squash Soup with Orzo)*

ZUPPA DI TRE ZUCCHE CON ORZO

# Three-Squash Soup with Orzo

MAKES 2½ QUARTS

*Orzo is better known as pearl barley and is a favorite addition to soups. It is just right in this glorious and hearty soup made with chunks of butternut and zucchini squash. Pureed spaghetti squash and cherry tomatoes are used to thicken the soup, giving it lots of flavor and texture. An added bonus is that the soup is very low in fat. Prepare the soup ingredients a day ahead by baking and pureeing the spaghetti squash, pureeing the tomatoes, and cutting up the vegetables.*

1¼ pounds spaghetti squash, cut in half, seeded, and cut into quarters

4½ cups water

1 tablespoon butter

1 pound leeks, white part only, washed well, cut in half lengthwise, and cut into ¼-inch-thick slices

2 zucchini (12 ounces total), cut in half lengthwise, then cut into ¼-inch-thick slices

1¼ pounds butternut squash, peeled, cut in half, seeded, and cut into ¼-inch pieces

4 cups pureed cherry tomatoes (2 pounds)

1 cup hot water

3½ teaspoons salt

¾ cup orzo or other small soup pasta

6 to 8 fresh basil leaves, minced

Preheat the oven to 375°F.

Place the spaghetti squash quarters cut side down in a baking pan with ½ cup of the water. Cover the pan with aluminum foil and bake until the squash is soft, about 30 minutes. When cool enough to handle, scoop the pulp from the cavity and transfer it to a food processor or blender. Puree the squash until smooth (you may have to do it in batches). There should be about 1½ cups. Transfer the squash to a bowl, cover, and refrigerate until ready to use. (Can be prepared a day or two ahead.)

While the squash is baking, melt the butter in a soup pot, add the leeks, and cook, covered, over low heat for 3 minutes, stirring a few times. Add the zucchini and butternut squash, stir to evenly mix the vegetables, cover the pot, and continue to cook over low heat for about 12 minutes. The vegetables should

retain their shape and be *al dente* but cooked. Stir in the tomatoes, hot water, pureed squash, and 2 teaspoons of the salt. Cover and cook over low heat for 10 minutes.

Meanwhile, bring the remaining 4 cups water to a boil, stir in the remaining 1½ teaspoons salt and the orzo and cook until the orzo is *al dente*, about 10 minutes. Drain and stir the orzo into the soup. Stir in the basil and serve.

TIP: Using a nonstick soup pot in this recipe eliminates the need to add much fat when cooking the leeks and vegetables.

NOTE: *Spaghetti squash can be cooked in a microwave on high power for 5 to 6 minutes per pound. Be sure to pierce the rind first before microwaving to prevent an explosion.*

ZUPPA DI GNOCCHETTI E SCAROLA

# Gnocchi and Escarole Soup

MAKES 2 QUARTS

*To me, tiny cuts of macaroni such as gnocchetti, shell-shaped pasta used in this recipe, will always be synonymous with comfort food. In an Italian kitchen it was the role of soup not only to satisfy but to soothe and heal, especially when one had a cold or an upset stomach. In this filling soup the goal is a balance of flavors, which come together beautifully.*

*Any type of dried bean can be used, but if you are really pressed for time, canned beans can be substituted if they are drained and rinsed well. Cooking the beans and pasta separately retains the texture of each ingredient.*

| | |
|---|---|
| 1 cup dried red kidney beans, picked over | 1 pound escarole, washed, drained, and coarsely chopped (see Tip) |
| 7 cups water | ½ teaspoon celery salt |
| 2 teaspoons fine sea salt | 3 cups hot Homemade Beef Broth (page 45) or Veal Stock (page 46) |
| 1 cup gnocchetti, orzo, or ditalini | 1 tablespoon tomato paste |
| ¼ pound pancetta or bacon, diced | Grinding of black pepper |
| 1 large leek (8 ounces), white part only, washed well and thinly sliced | Rinds of Parmigiano-Reggiano cheese |

Soak the beans overnight in 2 cups of the water. Next day, drain the beans, put them in a 2-quart saucepan, cover them with water, bring them to a boil, and continue to let them boil until just *al dente*, 8 to 10 minutes. Drain the beans, reserving 2 cups of the cooking water, place them in a large bowl, and set aside.

Refill the saucepan with the remaining 5 cups water, bring to a boil, stir in 1 teaspoon of the salt and the gnocchetti and cook over medium-high heat until just *al dente*. Drain and add the gnocchetti to the kidney beans.

In a soup pot, slowly brown the pancetta over medium heat, stirring often until it softens and begins to render some of its fat. Add the sliced leek and cook,

stirring occasionally, until soft. Stir in the escarole, remaining teaspoon salt, celery salt, stock, reserved cooking water, tomato paste, pepper, and cheese rinds. Cover the pot, bring the mixture to a boil, and cook over medium heat for 5 minutes. Uncover the pot, stir in the kidney beans and gnocchetti, cover the pot, and cook 5 minutes longer before serving.

TIP: Clean escarole well by soaking it in cold water for 20 minutes, then drain and rinse again in a colander. This also works for leeks. Cut them in half lengthwise first.

TIP: When you can no longer grate the remaining Parmigiano cheese near the rind, add the rind to the soup pot along with the stock and water. At the end of the cooking time, remove the rinds, scrape off the softened cheese, discarding the rind, and stir it back into the soup.

NOTE: *The soup can be made several days ahead but will thicken as it stands. Reheat it, adding warm water if a thinner consistency is desired.*

BRODO DI MANZO

# Homemade Beef Broth

MAKES 2½ TO 3 QUARTS

*Whenever I trim meat I save the bones in a plastic bag, and when I have enough I make beef broth. I do the same with chicken that I have deboned.*

1 pound beef shin

1 pound beef brisket

2 or 3 beef neck bones

1½ pounds chicken parts

1 tablespoon coarse sea salt

4 to 5 sprigs fresh Italian parsley

5 sprigs fresh thyme

1 bay leaf

2 red onions, peeled and cut in half

2 carrots, peeled and quartered

2 ribs celery with leaves, cut in half

2 fresh plum tomatoes, coarsely chopped

5 black peppercorns

Put all the meat and the chicken pieces in a large stockpot, add the salt, and cover with cold water. Bring to a boil and skim the foam that collects on the surface with a slotted spoon.

Tie the parsley, thyme, and bay leaf together with kitchen string and add it to the pot. Reduce the heat to medium, add the remaining ingredients, and stir with a wooden spoon. Let the broth simmer for 2½ to 3 hours. (The chicken will cook faster than the other meats; remove it when tender, after about an hour. Let

cool, and remove the meat from the bones to use in another dish.) As the broth cooks, skim off the foam that collects on the surface.

When the meat is tender, remove it along with the bones and reserve for another use. Pour the broth and vegetables into a colander lined with damp cheesecloth set over another pot. Press on the solids with the back of a spoon to release all the juices. Discard the solids. The broth is ready to use. It can be refrigerated for up to 1 week or frozen for up to 3 months.

CONSUMATO DI VITELLO

# Veal Stock

MAKES 1½ QUARTS

*Homemade veal stock lends rich flavor to many sauces and pasta-based dishes and is very simple to make. Whenever I buy inexpensive veal shoulder for stew, I save the bones trimmed from the meat and, when there is enough, make this delicious stock, which can be frozen for up to 3 months.*

Olive oil spray

2 pounds veal bones

1 large carrot, peeled and quartered

1 large onion, unpeeled and quartered

2 large cloves garlic, peeled

1 large bay leaf

1 rib celery, cut in half

1 cup hot water

Fine sea salt to taste

1 teaspoon cracked black peppercorns

Preheat the oven to 350°F. Generously coat the bottom of a roasting pan with olive oil spray. Add all the ingredients to the pan except the water, salt, and pepper and roast, turning the ingredients occasionally, until all the veal pieces are nicely browned, about 45 minutes. Transfer all the ingredients to a soup pot.

Pour the water into the roasting pan and with a wooden spoon scrape up any browned bits remaining in the pan. Add this liquid to the soup pot along with enough water to just cover the ingredients. Bring to a boil, reduce the heat to medium-low, and let simmer, covered, for 30 minutes.

Remove the bones and strain the stock through a cheesecloth-lined colander set over a bowl. Press hard on the solids with a wooden spoon to extract all the juices. Discard the solids. Season the stock with salt and pepper. The stock is ready to use or cover and refrigerate for up to 3 days or freeze for several months.

# Pasta Sauces

Sauces (*salse*) are flavor enhancers that unify a dish and make it complete, and pasta epitomizes the need for sauces because, without them, pasta is dead on a plate. There are hundreds of sauces, some as uncomplicated as the classic *aglio e olio* (garlic and oil) and some as complex and intense as a Bolognese ragù (meat sauce). But the one sauce the world defines as pasta's permanent partner is tomato sauce. Its place in the history of Italian gastronomy took hold in the nineteenth century in Naples, where the process of drying pasta was also successfully begun. Combining the two was the perfect marriage. When the waves of southern Italians came to America's shores in 1890, 1900, and 1910, they brought with them the art of creating what would become recognized here as their national dish, *maccheroni al pummarola* (macaroni with tomato sauce). But long before the tomato was considered safe to eat and embraced by southern Italians, pasta was often combined with sugar, bread crumbs, cheese, olive oil, or pounded nut sauces. Consider a recipe from the manuscript *Libro di cucina del secolo xlv,* translated by Ludivico Frati, in which a lasagne layered with a pesto of almonds is sprinkled with spices and sugar before serving. Or the old culinary tradition still practiced today in Salemi, Sicily, for the feast of St. Joseph, where cooked spaghetti is tossed with olive oil and sprinkled with toasted bread crumbs and sugar. Some say that the bread-crumb topping is symbolic of wood shavings because St. Joseph was a carpenter.

The point is that there are no standard sauces in Italian cuisine; they are as individual as the circumstances and people who create them. This was also true for my immigrant ancestors. My mother and grandmothers always made tomato sauce with meats that needed simmering for a long time and they always added sugar and sometimes tomato paste. But other family members eliminated tomato paste, or sugar, and often substituted wine for water.

Differences in sauces for pasta change from town to town and region to region within Italy, the raw products cultivated from north to south providing the ingredients for them. The rich dairy lands of

Lombardia and Emilia-Romagna result in wonderful butter and cheese sauces as well as long-simmered ragù; the clovelike smell of pesto made from delicate basil leaves and extra virgin olive oil can lead us only to Liguria, and Genoa in particular; and the rich volcanic ash offered up by Mount Vesuvius in Naples in the region of Campania yields juicy plum tomatoes, sturdy eggplant, sweet and hot peppers, and other vegetables, all used to make various types of sauces. Nontraditional sauces began to take their place too in Italy as *alta cucina* (gourmet cooking) developed to meet the expectations of the sophisticated tourist.

Though there are no rules for making sauces, there are guidelines for how to dress different types of pasta with sauce. The guide I like to use is this: if the pasta is a thin, long type like vermicelli or spaghetti, use a light, smooth sauce like garlic and oil, or a meatless tomato sauce that evenly coats the strands of pasta. If the pasta is a short chunky cut, like fusilli or rigatoni, use a heavier sauce like a ragù or a vegetable or walnut sauce so that bits of the ingredients can cling to and invade all the little crevices of the pasta, which is why macaroni shapes were created in the first place.

Some sauces can be prepared ahead and frozen successfully. This is especially true for tomato sauces, both with meat and meatless, as well as vegetable sauces. Freezing pesto sauce is not recommended. Some people make and freeze it without the cheese, adding the cheese after the pesto defrosts, but I find the texture and taste are a bit off with the basil becoming too sharp. Instead of freezing homemade pesto, try storing it in jars in your refrigerator (see the recipe on page 64). Pesto sauce will keep refrigerated up to 1 week if covered with a thin layer of olive oil.

## SALSA DI BESCIAMELLA

# Basic White Sauce

MAKES 4 CUPS

*Besciamella, white sauce, is more frequently associated with northern Italian cooking and is used in oven-baked pasta dishes like lasagne, or with vegetables or fish. It can be made ahead and refrigerated for 3 or 4 days but will thicken as it sits. As you reheat it, thin the sauce, if you wish, with a little milk. The basic recipe does not have the addition of herbs or spices. Those ingredients should be added after the sauce is cooked and should be tailored to the dish being prepared.*

½ cup (1 stick) unsalted butter
½ cup unbleached all-purpose flour
4 cups hot milk

Fine sea salt to taste
Ground white pepper to taste

In a large saucepan, melt the butter over medium-low heat; do not let the butter brown. Whisk in the flour and cook it until a uniform paste is formed and no streaks of flour remain. Slowly whisk in the milk in a steady stream. Cook about 10 minutes, stirring slowly until the sauce coats the back of a wooden spoon. Season with salt and pepper.

SALSA AGLIO E OLIO

# Garlic and Oil Sauce

MAKES 1 CUP

*When there is no time to cook, I resort to this garlic-and-olive-oil sauce for spaghetti or linguine. With all the ingredients on hand, this can be ready in less than 10 minutes, just enough time to boil the pasta. Use a fruity extra virgin olive oil for its intense flavor and cook the garlic slowly in it so it does not brown.*

⅔ cup extra virgin olive oil

2 cloves garlic, finely minced

1 teaspoon fine sea salt

⅓ cup minced fresh Italian parsley leaves

12 ounces spaghetti or linguine

Freshly grated Parmigiano-Reggiano or
 Pecorino cheese (optional)

Heat the olive oil slowly in a sauté pan over low heat and when it begins to shimmer, add the garlic and cook gently until it becomes soft but not brown, about 2 minutes. Turn off the heat, stir in the salt and parsley, and cover the pan.

Cook the pasta as directed on page 29 and drain, reserving ⅓ cup of the cooking water. Add the water to the garlic and oil and stir to blend. Quickly mix in the cooked pasta. Transfer the pasta to a platter or bowl and serve immediately with a sprinkling of cheese if desired.

NOTE: *To have parsley on hand when you need it, wash and dry a large bunch. Take the leaves off the stems. Discard the stems and mince the leaves with a chef's knife. Wrap the parsley in paper towels, place in airtight sandwich bags, and freeze. Take out what you need as you need it. This saves having to throw out unused parsley that wilts and dries out in the refrigerator.*

# Spaghetti Supper in Santa Caterina Villarmosa

The small, slim book was brittle and brown with age. Gingerly, I fingered the pages of this treasure, my grandfather Rosario Saporito's Italian passport. It had been given to me by my Aunt Phoebe Zampini for safekeeping. Issued during the reign of King Vittorio Emanuele III, it piqued my curiosity and I dreamed of a trip to Sicily someday, to the province of Caltanisetta, right in the center of the island, to visit my grandfather's town.

When the opportunity presented itself, I finally arrived in the mountainous town of Santa Caterina Villarmosa, my grandfather's birthplace and home until he was twenty-five. The day was overcast, which only enhanced the grayness of the buildings. I knew that most of this town had been heavily bombed during the war, destroying much of its original architecture, but it still had some of the typical places one finds in travels in Italy; the bar was the center of activity, the meeting place for an espresso or *acqua minerale,* and out-side the bar the men of the town sat in their hats and coats playing cards and drinking wine. The local vegetable store and pastry shop were busy, too, and a small hardware store advertised *cucuzza,* squash seeds. In the town center stood a dry-as-a-bone water fountain and stone monument depicting a worker with his lunchbox in hand, coming home to greet his wife and child. This representation in stone spoke volumes to me in terms of *la famiglia* (the family), always the most important thing to an Italian.

The first thing I decided to do was to get myself oriented. As I walked around, I was overcome with emotion to think that I had come full circle in the history of my family, the Saporito family. Once my grandfather lived here, worked here, and knew his neighbors. Then one day he had enough, crossed the mountains, and came by ship to America because he had a dream and it was full of new hope in a new world. Now I had come back, hoping for some answers to the kind of life he led here. I knew of no remaining relatives in the town and as I walked toward the *municipio* (town hall), I felt the inquisitive eyes of onlookers all around me. It was obvi-ous that this town was not a tourist destination. The town office was closed, so I walked to the small *biblioteca* (library), where a woman greeted me and, in my fumbling Italian (which bore no resemblance to the Sicilian dialect), I introduced myself and showed her the passport.

*"L'informazione, signora, per favore. Conosce lei il nome Saporito?"* She smiled and studied the passport, then called out to a young man in the back and I heard a friendly, "Can I help you?" "English, you speak English," I blurted out and Antonio Fiaccato introduced himself to me as a self-appointed researcher in the library. "Yes, of course, Saporito, it is a common name in this town; there are many; we just buried Giuseppe Saporito yesterday. Come with me to the Chiesa Madre (mother church); we will look up the records of your family. *Va bene?"*

Expecting a computer printout of my grandfather's life in this town, I quickened my pace and followed Antonio to the church, hanging on every word he spoke as he detailed the life in the town. "How is it that you speak English?" "Ah, I have studied in school and now I write plays; I am doing research about the catacombs under the Chiesa Madre where hundreds of people are buried."

In the church, women were preparing the altar for Palm Sunday and the smell of lilies filled the air. We walked to the back of the church into a small room full of dusty books; so much for computer-generated information, I thought. With deft hands Antonio fingered the books.

"*Ah, qua* [here]," he said, pointing out the information. "You see the name of your grandfather and the day he was baptized, and your great-grandfather and great-grandmother, they are buried under the church. Your great-grandmother was an Alonghi and she was related to the first parish priest [1606]."

I felt like a detective in an old Nancy Drew story; we sat for what seemed like hours collecting information; I was being given a treasure . . . my heritage.

Antonio was so gracious to spend all that time with me that I wanted to repay him in some way; take him to a *ristorante,* give him some money; I felt so indebted, but he seized the moment and surprised me by saying, "Today you must have dinner with me, my mother, and grandmother . . . you are a Saporito, so you are one of

us." Me sharing a meal in a Sicilian home in my grandfather's town with people I did not even know . . . could this be real?

I arrived with Antonio in a small winding street with entryways blocking out the world only by long colorful roping, no doors. Antonio parted the ropes to his grandmother's modest home and there stood a petite woman in a frayed apron with a topknot of gray hair and a worn gentle face that told the story of a hard life. She was filling a pot with water for spaghetti. I started to shake her hand but she grabbed me and kissed me on both cheeks. I knew I was as welcome as any longtime friend.

The room was small, no bigger than a small bedroom, and yet it felt cozy and inviting. Antonio's mother arrived by bus from Caltanisetta to help his grandmother cook and I felt uneasy thinking that they were going to all this trouble for a stranger, especially when I spied the cutlets, pork sausage, roasted artichokes, potatoes, and salad. From the appearance of the humble surroundings, I was sure that they did not eat this way every day. Antonio was proud of the fact that he had made the tomato sauce for the spaghetti, which was a thicker cut

called bucatini or perciatelli. This was surprising, since the kitchen in Sicily is the realm of *le donne* (the women). When the bucatini was nearly ready, Antonio tested it for tenderness. "*Ah, basta sono cotti*" (enough, they are cooled). Draining them fogged up the entire room. The pasta went into a bowl and the sauce and several huge leaves of fragrant basil were mixed in. We crowded around the table and the bucatini was served with clumps of fresh sheep's milk ricotta cheese, which Antonio's mother buys from a nearby farm.

I have eaten bucatini hundreds of times but this was *really* the first time because of the experience and significance that was attached to the moment. I raised my glass to the cooks, "*Complimenti,*" and I imagined that if my Grandfather Rosario Saporito were there, too, he would have done the same.

## SALSA DI POMODORO E BASILICO

# Tomato and Basil Sauce

MAKES 9½ TO 10 CUPS

*Canned tomato sauce will never measure up to homemade, a relatively simple undertaking that is much less costly than buying jarred types, which are too full of insipid dried herbs, and high in sodium and preservatives. If you want to make fresh tomato sauce, consider using plum varieties such as Roma or San Marzano for their sweetness and meatiness. If you are using canned plum tomatoes, choose those that are imported from Italy. Cherry tomatoes, known as pomodorini in Italy, can also be used; this is a common practice in Puglia. In addition to the tomatoes, use a good extra virgin olive oil that is not too fruity, or it will overwhelm the tomato flavor. The rest of the ingredients are the cook's whim; some begin with a battuto, a finely minced combination of celery, onion, garlic, and carrots. These are the odori, or flavor enhancers, which are cooked first in the olive oil before adding the tomatoes. Others sauté only onions and garlic in olive oil, then add tomatoes, fresh basil, salt, pepper, sometimes a pinch of sugar, and a little red wine. To make a spicy tomato sauce, hot red pepper, either fresh or in dried flake form, is added.*

*An important thing to remember is that meatless tomato sauce does not need to cook for very long, 15 minutes at most. Tomato sauces that simmer for hours usually have the addition of a tough cut of meat such as round steak, spare ribs, or a combination of meats that is then served at the secondo, the second course.*

*The following recipe is a basic all-purpose meatless sauce. It can be made in large quantities and frozen for months. Use the sauce on pasta, with meat, fowl, or fish, and for pizza and calzones.*

5 pounds ripe plum tomatoes or three 28-ounce cans crushed plum tomatoes with their liquid

½ cup extra virgin olive oil

⅔ cup diced onion

3 cloves garlic, minced

1½ cups dry red wine

¼ cup sugar

1 tablespoon fine sea salt or to taste

Freshly ground black pepper to taste

6 to 8 large sprigs fresh basil

If using fresh tomatoes, core them, cut them into coarse chunks, and puree them in a food processor, blender, or food mill until smooth. Strain the fresh or canned tomatoes through a fine sieve to remove the skins and seeds. Set aside.

Heat the olive oil in a large pot and cook the onion over medium heat, stirring, until soft. Add the garlic and cook, stirring occasionally, until it becomes soft. Do not let the garlic brown or an acrid taste will be imparted to the sauce. Pour in the tomatoes and wine and stir to combine. Add the remaining ingredients, reduce the heat to low, and simmer until thickened, about 15 minutes.

POMODORO MOZZARELLA ED ACCIUGATA

# Tomato, Cheese, and Anchovy Sauce

*This spicy tomato-and-anchovy sauce is the perfect accompaniment for plain fusilli.*

FOR THE PASTA

4 to 6 quarts water

2 tablespoons salt

1 pound homemade (page 26) or store-bought
  fusilli

1 tablespoon extra virgin olive oil

FOR THE SAUCE

*(makes about 2 cups)*

2 tablespoons extra virgin olive oil

3 anchovy fillets in salt, rinsed and dried

2 ounces green olives in brine, drained, pitted,
  and diced

1¾ cups Tomato and Basil Sauce (opposite)

5 ounces fresh mozzarella (*fior di latte*), diced

Fine sea salt to taste

Grinding of black pepper

¾ teaspoon dried oregano

Bring the water to a boil in a pasta pot with an insert. Add the salt and fusilli. For commercially prepared fusilli, follow the directions on page 29. For homemade, the cooking time will be less but more than for most types of homemade pasta because of their thickness. Cook until *al dente*, 4 to 5 minutes. Drain the fusilli and place them in a large bowl. Toss with the 1 tablespoon olive oil, cover, and set aside.

Heat the 2 tablespoons olive oil in a medium-size saucepan over low heat, stir in the anchovies with a wooden spoon, and cook until they almost dissolve into the oil. Stir in the olives and tomato sauce, bring the ingredients to a boil, and cook for 2 minutes. Stir in the mozzarella, pour the sauce over the fusilli, and mix everything together very quickly, allowing the cheese to melt. Add the salt, pepper, and oregano, toss again, and transfer the mixture to a pasta platter. Serve immediately.

## SALSA DI POMODORO CRUDO

# Uncooked Tomato Sauce

MAKES 2 CUPS

*The juxtaposition of hot against cool is perfect in this classic uncooked tomato sauce for both fresh and dried pasta. My advice is to make this sauce with abandon when tomatoes are in season and preferably from your own garden. For maximum flavor, the sauce needs to marinate a least 6 hours or, even better, prepare the sauce 2 days ahead and refrigerate it. Bring to room temperature before using. Use the sauce on a pound of short-cut pasta like rigatoni, penne, fusilli, or orecchiette.*

½ cup extra virgin olive oil

2 large cloves garlic, peeled

7 or 8 large fresh basil leaves, stemmed

⅓ cup tightly packed fresh Italian parsley leaves, stems removed

1 pound (about 4) meaty plum tomatoes

1 teaspoon fine sea salt

1½ tablespoons sugar

Freshly ground black pepper to taste

2 teaspoons balsamic vinegar

Pour the olive oil into a large glass bowl and set aside. With a chef's knife, mince the garlic, basil, and parsley together and add to the olive oil.

Fill a 1-quart saucepan with water and bring to a boil. Drop the tomatoes into the water and blanch them just until the skins begin to split, no more than a minute. Remove the tomatoes with a slotted spoon to a cutting board and let cool. Peel away the skins and discard. Core the tomatoes, seed them if you wish, dice, and add them to the bowl with the olive oil mixture.

Mix in the salt, sugar, pepper, and balsamic vinegar. Cover the bowl with plastic wrap and let marinate before serving over hot pasta.

POMODORO SECCO ED ACCIUGATA

# Dried Tomato and Anchovy Sauce

MAKES 1 CUP

*When I make dried tomato and anchovy sauce, I am transported to the sunny, arid landscape of central Sicily, where the ritual of making estrattu, a concentrated tomato paste prepared by laboriously stirring tomatoes for hours in the intense Sicilian sun, happens every summer. The process eliminates the moisture of the tomatoes, and just a little of the final concentrate is enough to wake up a simmering stew, or breathe new life into a common tomato sauce. But one must be realistic and adapt, as in this concentrated sauce made from dried tomatoes in olive oil. The flavor is intense and just a little goes a long way. Buy quality dried tomatoes in extra virgin olive oil or make your own dried tomatoes in olive oil with the help of a dehydrator or by drying them in your oven with very low heat. This sauce is best used on short, chunky types of pasta like rigatoni, radiatore, wheels, ziti, or fusilli. One-half cup of this concentrated sauce, mixed with a little of the pasta cooking water, is enough to dress a pound of pasta. The sauce will keep a long time under refrigeration (2 to 3 weeks) if covered with a thin layer of olive oil.*

¼ cup extra virgin olive oil

2 large cloves garlic, minced

4 anchovy fillets in olive oil, drained
and chopped

1 tablespoon capers in salt, rinsed

1 cup drained Dried Tomatoes in Olive Oil
homemade (page 56), or store-bought

¼ cup dry red wine

Heat the olive oil over low heat in a sauté pan, add the garlic and anchovies, and stir with a wooden spoon until the anchovies dissolve into the oil. Add the capers, tomatoes, and wine and cook for 2 minutes, stirring often. Transfer the mixture to a food processor or blender and pulse until the tomatoes are pureed.

Transfer the mixture to a jar and cover with a thin layer of extra virgin olive oil. Then cap tightly and refrigerate. When ready to use, scoop out the desired amount and heat slowly in a saucepan. Cover the remaining sauce again with a thin layer of olive oil and refrigerate.

NOTE: *This sauce is also good on pizza and spread on slices of toasted bread* (bruschetta).

## POMODORI SECCHI SOTT'OLIO

# Dried Tomatoes in Olive Oil

MAKES TWO 12-OUNCE JARS

*Dried tomatoes in olive oil have exquisite flavor, and what a gift to give yourself in the stillness of winter. Plum or cherry tomatoes work best and the "putting up" should be done during gardening season when tomatoes are at peak flavor. They store beautifully for months. Use them diced as a sauce for pasta, in salads, and for antipasto.*

14 unblemished meaty plum tomatoes, washed and dried

3 cups red wine vinegar

Two 12-ounce jars and lids, sterilized

8 fresh basil leaves

3 tablespoons capers in salt, rinsed and diced

2 tablespoons black peppercorns

2 teaspoons fine sea salt

2 to 2½ cups extra virgin olive oil, as needed

Core and cut the tomatoes in half lengthwise.

Place the tomatoes cut side down in a dehydrator and dry according to the manufacturer's directions. Or place cut side down on wire racks set on baking sheets in a preheated 225°F oven. Let dry until they have the texture of dried apricots. This may take a day or longer, depending on the size of the tomatoes.

Pour the wine vinegar into a large nonreactive saucepan and bring to a boil. Add the tomatoes and blanch them for 1 minute. Remove the tomatoes with a slotted spoon and drain well. The vinegar acts as a preservative and gives added flavor to the tomatoes.

Layer the tomatoes into the sterilized jars, adding half the basil, capers, peppercorns, and salt to each jar.

Slowly pour the olive oil into the jars, pressing down on the tomatoes slightly with a wooden spoon. Make sure that the tomatoes are completely submerged under the oil at all times, or they will be exposed to air and potential bacteria growth. Cap the jars tightly and place them in a cool spot overnight. The next day, check the level of the oil and add more to the jars if the tomatoes are poking out of the oil. Check the jars two or three more times, adding more oil if necessary.

Recap the jars and store them in a cool place for 6 weeks before using. Refrigerate after opening and bring the tomatoes to room temperature before serving.

SALSA DI POMODORO E PORRO ARROSTITO

# Roasted Tomato and Leek Sauce

MAKES 1½ CUPS SMOOTH OR 2¼ CUPS CHUNKY

*I often surprise myself by taking little detours with cooking techniques and traditions. Such is the case with this roasted no-fat tomato-and-leek sauce. The sauce can be smooth or chunky and dress fresh, filled, or plain pasta. A favorite combination with the smooth version of this sauce is spaghetti with sugar snap peas and Sardinian feta cheese (page 87). Use the chunky version with rigatoni or with orecchiette.*

1½ pounds fresh plum tomatoes, washed, cored, and left whole

1 large leek (6 ounces), white part only, cut lengthwise, washed well, and cut into quarters

1½ teaspoons fine sea salt

2 teaspoons dried oregano

1 tablespoon balsamic vinegar

1 tablespoon sugar

Preheat the oven to 350°F.

Place the whole tomatoes and the leek (cut side down) on a nonstick baking sheet. Roast the vegetables until the tomatoes are soft to the touch and the leek has begun to brown, 30 to 35 minutes. Transfer the vegetables to a food processor and process until a thick, chunky sauce is obtained.

To make a smooth sauce, transfer the pureed vegetables to a fine mesh colander placed over a bowl.

Press on the ingredients with a wooden spoon to squeeze the sauce through the colander. Discard the solids.

Transfer the sauce to a large nonreactive bowl and stir in the salt, oregano, vinegar, and sugar. The sauce is ready to use, or freeze for future use.

SALSA DI OLIVA

# Olive Sauce

MAKES 1½ CUPS

*It is written that the olive is a gift from the gods. Certainly no food is more revered than the oil extracted from this ancient fruit that is known today for its health benefits as well as its culinary fame. In this no-cook olive sauce two types of olives, Kalamata and Cerignola, are blended together to make a piquant sauce that is sensational not only on pasta like the Pici #1 on page 18 but on fish, bruschetta, and pizza and mixed into bread dough. The intensity of the flavors allows one to use the sauce sparingly (½ cup will sauce about ½ pound of pasta) and it will keep for a couple of weeks in the refrigerator if the top is covered with a thin layer of olive oil. If you do not have an olive pitter to remove the pits, use a wide-bottomed jar to smash each olive; this easily removes the pit.*

½ pound Kalamata olives, pitted

½ pound Cerignola olives, pitted

3 cloves garlic, peeled

⅓ cup fresh Italian parsley leaves, stems removed

2 tablespoons fresh thyme leaves

¼ cup extra virgin olive oil

½ teaspoon fine sea salt

½ teaspoon coarsely ground black pepper

Place the olives and garlic in the bowl of a food processor and pulse for 10 seconds. Add the parsley and thyme and pulse again for 10 seconds. With the motor running, add the olive oil through the feed tube in a slow stream. The sauce should look finely minced and have some texture to it. Transfer the sauce to a bowl and stir in the salt and black pepper.

Store the sauce in a jar in the refrigerator. Bring the jar to room temperature when ready to use. After removing some of the sauce, pour a thin layer of olive oil over the top to prevent air from getting in and allowing bacteria to grow.

## Variation

Add julienned roasted sweet red and yellow peppers after mixing the pasta with the sauce and a few coarsely chopped black oil-cured olives for color and contrast.

NOTE: *If you prefer a hot-tasting olive sauce, add 1 teaspoon dried red pepper flakes to the sauce.*

*Pici (page 18) served with
Salsa di Oliva (Olive Sauce)*

SALSA DI CARCIOFO

# Artichoke Sauce

MAKES ABOUT 2¼ CUPS

*Watching the "artichoke lady" of Verona whittle away the outer leaves of bushels of artichokes like a master woodcarver was the inspiration for this quick artichoke sauce using canned artichoke hearts. If you wish to use fresh artichokes, you will need 4 large ones. This sauce is delicious over spaghetti or linguine. Try the spicy version on page 61, which can also be prepared ahead of time.*

3 tablespoons extra virgin olive oil

½ cup thinly sliced shallots (4 ounces)

1 medium-size onion, peeled and thinly sliced

3 cloves garlic, minced

One 14-ounce can artichoke hearts, drained, rinsed, and thinly sliced or 4 fresh cleaned artichoke hearts (see Note)

½ cup grated carrots

¼ teaspoon celery salt

½ teaspoon fine sea salt

½ teaspoon dried oregano

¼ teaspoon coarsely ground black pepper

¾ cup dry white wine

½ cup minced fresh Italian parsley leaves, stems removed

1 pound linguine

Freshly grated Parmigiano-Reggiano cheese to sprinkle

Heat the olive oil over medium heat in a large sauté pan, add the shallots and onion, and cook slowly, stirring occasionally, until the mixture begins to wilt but not turn brown. Stir in the garlic and cook until it softens but do not let it brown. Stir in the artichokes, carrots, celery salt, sea salt, oregano, and black pepper and cook for 2 minutes, stirring occasionally. Pour in the wine, increase the heat to high, and cook for 2 minutes, stirring occasionally. Stir in the parsley, cover the pan, and keep the sauce warm while the linguine cooks.

Cook the linguine according to the directions on page 29. When *al dente*, drain the pasta, reserving 2 tablespoons of the cooking water. Return the pasta

to the pot and, over low heat, stir in the artichoke sauce and the reserved cooking water. Mix well. Transfer to a pasta platter and serve immediately with grated cheese to pass.

NOTE: *To clean fresh artichokes, cut and discard the stem and remove the outer leaves until the pale yellow leaves appear. Cut off the top two thirds of the artichokes. Open the center and scrape out the hairy choke. Place the artichoke hearts in cold water with fresh lemon juice. Bring a pot of water to a boil, add the artichokes and boil until tender, 8 to 10 minutes. Drain and proceed with the recipe. Use a serrated knife to make neat artichoke slices.*

SALSA DI CARCIOFO ALLA CAMPAGNA
# Country-Style Artichoke Sauce

MAKES ABOUT 2½ CUPS

*The feisty flavor of this country-style artichoke sauce is a good choice for any short-cut type of pasta and can be made several days ahead and refrigerated. Since artichokes by themselves are mildly nutty in flavor, the capers, pungent olives, tomatoes, and pancetta make a compatible taste combination. When fresh artichokes are not in season or just too expensive, make this sauce using frozen artichoke hearts.*

One 9-ounce package frozen artichoke hearts (about 2 cups)

½ cup homemade (page 35) or canned low-sodium chicken broth

1 tablespoon extra virgin olive oil

2 ounces pancetta, diced

1 large clove garlic, minced

12 oil-cured black olives, pitted and diced

1 tablespoon capers in salt, rinsed and diced

½ pound cherry tomatoes, diced

½ teaspoon sea salt

Grinding of black pepper

1 tablespoon fresh lemon juice

Place the artichoke hearts in a saucepan with the chicken broth and bring to a boil. Reduce the heat to medium-high, cover the pan, and cook for 3 minutes. Uncover the pan and cook 2 minutes more. Drain the artichokes in a strainer set over a bowl. Reserve the liquid and, when cool, cut the artichoke hearts into coarse pieces and set aside.

Heat the olive oil in a medium-size sauté pan over medium heat, add the pancetta, and cook, stirring, until it begins to brown and give off its fat. Stir in the garlic and cook until it softens. Stir in the olives, reserved artichoke juice, capers, tomatoes, salt, pepper, lemon juice, and artichokes. Cook the sauce, covered, over medium heat for 5 minutes. Uncover and cook 2 minutes more. The sauce is ready to use.

## SALSA DI CIPOLLA E FUNGO CON ACETO BALSAMICO

# Onion, Mushroom, and Balsamic Vinegar Sauce

MAKES 2 CUPS

*What gives this onion-and-mushroom sauce such intense flavor is cooking the onion very slowly in a young balsamic vinegar such as produced by Fini, available in many supermarkets and Italian specialty stores. The sauce is delicious on both long and short cuts of dried pasta but I would not recommend it on filled pastas where its strong flavor would compete with the delicacy of the pasta and the filling. Sometimes I add a sprinkling of fresh parsley or thyme and shavings of Parmigiano-Reggiano cheese just before serving.*

1 large red Spanish onion, chopped

⅔ cup balsamic vinegar

2 tablespoons extra virgin olive oil

3½ cups sliced fresh portobello or button mushrooms (8 ounces)

Grinding of coarse black pepper

¼ teaspoon fine sea salt

1 pound pasta

⅓ cup minced fresh Italian parsley or thyme leaves (optional)

Shavings of Parmigiano-Reggiano cheese (optional)

In a medium-size nonreactive saucepan, combine the onion and vinegar and simmer the mixture, uncovered, until the onion is very soft and dark-colored and the liquid has thickened enough so that it is syrupy, about 15 minutes. Stir once or twice. Do not allow the liquid to completely evaporate; it will reduce in volume in cooking. Remove the saucepan from the heat and set aside.

Meanwhile, heat the olive oil in a large sauté pan, stir in the mushrooms, and cook over medium heat, stirring occasionally, until the mushrooms have softened and are just beginning to release their juices. Stir in the onion mixture, season with pepper and salt, and cook another 2 minutes.

Cook the pasta according to the directions on page 29. When *al dente*, drain it and transfer it to back to the pasta pot. Stir in the sauce and transfer the mixture to a serving platter. If desired, sprinkle the herbs and shavings of cheese over the top and serve.

## SALSA DI PREZZEMOLO, PATATE, ED ACETO BALSAMICO

# Parsley, Potato, and Balsamic Vinegar Sauce

MAKES ABOUT 1 CUP

*Cooked potato gives body to this sauce, which can be used on both short and long cuts of dried pasta. It is best made several hours ahead and kept at room temperature, and even though this is not a traditional sauce for pasta, it does make use of a very traditional condiment, aceto balsamico (balsamic vinegar). A word of caution about balsamic vinegar; there are many domestic imitations that are nothing more than wine vinegar to which caramel coloring and sugar have been added. True balsamic vinegar is made in Italy in Modena and Reggio from the unfermented cooked grape juice of the Trebbiano grape. The best aceto balsamico tradizionale is an artisan product that is aged for 12 to even 100 years in different types of wood casks and, when ready, is a dark mahogany color with the consistency of syrup that easily coats a glass; it has an intense flavor. A few drops can transform the flavor of a dish. It is made in accordance with government regulations, each bottle carrying a seal of authenticity. Look for the letters API MO (Modena) or API RE (Reggio) on the label of balsamic vinegars to verify that they are what they purport to be. For the most part, the balsamic vinegars sold here from Italy are young, five-year-old vinegars, referred to as aceto balsamico industriale. This recipe makes enough to dress ½ pound of dried pasta and is a good choice when there are only two for dinner.*

| | |
|---|---|
| 1 cup packed fresh Italian parsley leaves | 3 to 4 tablespoons extra virgin olive oil |
| 1 tablespoon capers in salt, rinsed and dried | ½ teaspoon fine sea salt |
| 1 medium-size potato, boiled until tender, peeled, and diced | 1½ tablespoons balsamic vinegar |
| | ½ pound pasta |

Place the parsley, capers, and potato in the bowl of a food processor and pulse to blend the ingredients until the parsley is reduced to flecks. With the motor running, pour the olive oil through the feed tube in a slow stream until a smooth sauce is obtained.

Transfer the sauce to a bowl. Season with the salt and stir in the balsamic vinegar. Cover and leave at room temperature for several hours. When ready to use, cook the pasta and while it is cooking slowly reheat the sauce until it is hot. Drain the pasta, then return it to the pasta pot and stir in the sauce. Transfer the pasta to a serving platter and serve immediately.

# Pesto Sauce

MAKES ABOUT ¾ CUP

*This classic Genovese pesto sauce is made from fresh basil leaves that are crushed in a mortar with a pestle. To save time, use a food processor. Blanch the basil leaves before grinding them to help preserve the sauce's green color.*

¼ cup pine nuts or walnuts

4 cups water

2 cups packed fresh basil leaves

1 teaspoon coarse sea salt

3 cloves garlic, peeled

½ cup extra virgin olive oil

3 tablespoons freshly grated Pecorino or Parmigiano-Reggiano cheese

Preheat the oven to 350°F. Spread the pine nuts on a baking sheet and toast them for 4 to 5 minutes, until they are golden brown. Transfer the nuts to a bowl to cool.

Bring the water to a boil in a medium-size saucepan, add the basil leaves, and blanch them for 1 minute. Remove the leaves with a slotted spoon to a clean kitchen towel. Blot the leaves dry, then transfer them to the bowl of a food processor or blender with the salt and garlic cloves. Pulse the mixture to grind up the ingredients. Add the pine nuts and pulse again until a uniform coarse mixture is obtained. With the motor running, slowly add the olive oil through the feed tube until a sauce consistency is obtained that is not too thin. Remove the pesto to a small bowl and stir in the cheese. Transfer the sauce to a jar. Pour a thin layer of olive oil over the top of the sauce. This will keep the sauce from turning brown. Cap the jar and store the sauce in the refrigerator until ready to use. The sauce will keep about 2 weeks in the refrigerator.

SALSA DI MENTA E NOCE

# Mint and Walnut Sauce

SERVES 4 TO 6

*This is a special pasta sauce from antiquity that the Etruscans from the town of Chiusi used to serve. Pici, a thin spaghetti, is excellent with this sauce, and the pasta as well as the sauce can be made in no time in a food processor. The pici can be dried for long storage as described on page 16.*

4 ounces walnut halves

1 cup packed fresh mint leaves, washed, dried, and stemmed

1 teaspoon fine sea salt

1 large clove garlic, peeled

6 tablespoons extra virgin olive oil

1 pound Pici (page 18)

Freshly grated Parmigiano-Reggiano cheese for sprinkling

Place the nuts, mint, salt, and garlic in the bowl of a food processor fitted with the steel blade. Process the mixture until the nuts and mint are finely minced. Add the olive oil through the feed tube a dribble at a time while the motor is running. Process until the sauce is blended and grainy in texture.

Cook the pici as described on page 30. While the pici are cooking, heat the sauce in a small saucepan over low heat. Drain the pici, reserving ¼ cup of the cooking water. Stir the water into the warm sauce.

Return the pici to the pasta pot, pour in the sauce, and stir over low heat until the sauce evenly coats the pici. Transfer the pici to a platter and serve with grated cheese.

NOTE: *The sauce can be made up to 1 week ahead and refrigerated.*

SALSA DELL'ERBE

# Herb Sauce

MAKES 1 CUP

*This quick herb sauce teamed with Sardinian feta cheese can be made several days ahead and is perfect on short cuts of pasta like fusilli. Do not substitute dried herbs for fresh as that would be the sauce's ruination. The flavor of this sauce is developed by the slow cooking of the herbs for just 1 minute so their delicate oils will not be destroyed.*

½ cup extra virgin olive oil

3 cloves garlic, peeled and cut in half lengthwise

6 scallions, white part only, cut into thin rounds

½ cup minced arugula leaves

½ cup minced fresh basil leaves

½ cup minced fresh Italian parsley leaves, without stems

1 teaspoon fine sea salt

1 pound homemade (page 26) or store-bought fusilli

½ pound feta cheese, crumbled

Heat the olive oil in a medium-size sauté pan over medium heat, add the garlic halves, and cook slowly, pressing on the cloves with a wooden spoon to flavor the oil. When the edges of the cloves begin to turn golden brown, remove and discard them.

Cook the scallions in the olive oil, stirring, until they soften. Stir in the arugula, basil, and parsley and cook slowly for 1 minute. Stir in the salt. Keep the sauce over low heat while the fusilli are cooking.

Cook the fusilli as directed on page 29. When *al dente*, drain the fusilli, reserving 2 tablespoons of the cooking water. Return the fusilli to the cooking pot, along with the reserved cooking water, add the sauce, and mix to evenly coat the fusilli. Transfer to a serving bowl or platter, sprinkle the feta cheese over the top, and serve.

TIP: Spray a chef's knife with vegetable or olive oil spray before mincing the herbs to prevent them from sticking to the knife blade.

NOTE: *The sauce will keep covered at room temperature for 3 days or may be refrigerated for longer storage.*

NOTE: *This is also a great marinade for fish or chicken.*

*Fusilli Casalinghi (Homemade Fusilli) (page 26) served with Salsa dell'Erbe (Herb Sauce)*

# Ragù alla Bolognese

MAKES 4½ CUPS

*A ragù is a slow-simmering meat sauce and is a classic of Bolognese cooking, with many variations. The long, slow cooking in an earthenware pot results in a hearty, dense sauce with intense flavor that is the perfect foil for chunky-style pasta such as rigatoni rigati (rigatoni with lines) or ziti, or as the filling for lasagne, or as the sauce for a layered tortellini timballo (mold) or pasticcio (pasta filled pie).*

2 ounces pancetta

1 small onion, peeled and quartered

1 medium-size carrot, peeled

1 medium-size rib celery

2 tablespoons extra-virgin olive oil

1 pound ground pork or beef

Fine sea salt to taste

¼ teaspoon freshly ground black pepper

½ cup dry red wine

14 ounces tomatoes, peeled and cut into pieces

½ cup milk or heavy cream

Mince the pancetta, onion, carrot, and celery together. Set aside.

Heat the olive oil in a medium-size earthenware, cast-iron, or other heavy-duty pot. Over low heat, cook the minced vegetable mixture very slowly, uncovered, for 30 minutes. Add the ground meat, salt, and pepper and brown the meat completely. Stir in the wine and let it completely evaporate. Stir in the tomatoes, cover the pot, and cook the ragù over very low heat for 45 minutes. Stir in the milk or cream and heat through.

# Meatless Pasta Dishes

## ZITI CON QUATTRO FORMAGGI
# Ziti with Four Cheeses

SERVES 4 TO 6

*Everyone has their favorite comfort food and mine is this rich and quick-to-make macaroni and cheese with four cheeses that is a specialty of the Hotel Belvedere Syrene in Sorrento. Instead of making a cream sauce, mixing in the pasta, and baking the dish in the oven, the cheeses are added directly to the hot pasta and stirred over low heat to melt them and served immediately. Use a short cut of pasta such as ziti, rigatoni, or medium shells.*

5 tablespoons unsalted butter

½ cup fresh bread crumbs

1 pound ziti

½ cup diced Fontina cheese

½ cup diced fresh mozzarella cheese

½ cup diced Asiago cheese

½ cup freshly grated Parmigiano-Reggiano cheese

¼ teaspoon freshly grated nutmeg

Fine sea salt to taste

½ cup heavy cream

To "toast" the bread crumbs heat 1 tablespoon of the butter in a small sauté pan, add the bread crumbs, and cook them until golden brown. Transfer the crumbs to a small bowl and set aside.

Cook the ziti according to the directions on page 29. Drain and return to the pasta pot. Over low heat, stir the ziti with the remaining 4 tablespoons butter until it is well coated. Scatter the Fontina, mozzarella, and Asiago cheeses over the top and let them remain on top for 1 to 2 minutes to warm over low heat. Stir vigorously with a wooden spoon to melt the cheeses, then stir in the Parmigiano, nutmeg, salt, and heavy cream until well mixed.

Transfer the macaroni and cheese to a serving platter. Sprinkle the toasted bread crumbs over the top and serve immediately.

PERCIATELLI CON PAN GRATTUGIATO
# Thick Spaghetti with Bread Crumbs

SERVES 4 TO 6

*Perciatelli is similar to spaghetti but thicker and hollow. It is also called bucatini and is very popular in southern Italy. In Salemi, Sicily, I ate perciatelli on the feast of St. Joseph, the carpenter, served with "toasted" bread crumbs that had been tossed with a little sugar. Some say that the bread crumbs are symbolic of the wood shavings of a carpenter and the sugar is always an ingredient because on the feast, the Holy Family, often portrayed by children, are the first to eat this dish. A coarse-type bread makes the best crumbs; soft bread will not have enough texture and crunch to hold up when tossed with the cooked pasta. Serve as a first course followed by roasted chicken or capon.*

6 tablespoons extra virgin olive oil

1½ cups coarse fresh bread crumbs

1 tablespoon sugar

1 pound perciatelli or spaghetti

1½ teaspoons fine sea salt

Heat 2 tablespoons of the olive oil in a large sauté pan. Add the bread crumbs and stir with a wooden spoon to coat them with the oil. Cook the crumbs over medium heat, stirring occasionally, until they are golden brown in color. Remove the crumbs to a bowl, stir in the sugar, and set aside.

Cook the perciatelli according to the instructions on page 29. Drain the pasta, reserving 2 tablespoons of the cooking water.

Return the pasta to the cooking pot, stir in the water, the remaining ¼ cup olive oil, and the salt. Transfer the pasta to a platter. Sprinkle half of the bread crumbs over the top and, with two spoons, toss the pasta to evenly coat the strands with the crumbs. Sprinkle the remaining crumbs over the top and serve immediately.

# Trenette with Pesto, Potatoes, and Green Beans

SERVES 4 TO 6

*This recipe combines pasta from Liguria called trenette and pesto with potatoes and green beans, and is a specialty found in Cinque Terre and Portofino. Linguine can be used instead of the home-made trenette.*

4 to 6 quarts water

1 tablespoon salt

2 medium-size potatoes, peeled and diced

½ pound green beans, trimmed and cut into 1-inch diagonal pieces

1 pound Trenette (page 19)

½ cup Pesto Sauce (page 64)

Freshly grated Pecorino or Parmigiano-Reggiano cheese for sprinkling

Bring the water to a boil in a pasta pot. Add the salt, potatoes, and green beans and cook until the vegetables are *al dente*, tender but still firm, about 4 minutes. Add the pasta, stir it with a pasta fork, cover the pot, and bring the water back to a boil. Uncover the pot and cook the pasta just until *al dente*, about 3 minutes. Drain the pasta and vegetables into a colander, reserving ½ cup of the cooking water. Return the pasta and vegetables to the pot.

In a small bowl, combine the prepared pesto sauce with just enough of the reserved cooking water to make a smooth consistency. Pour the sauce over the pasta. Gently combine and mix the ingredients well over low heat. Transfer the pasta and vegetables to a platter or bowl and serve immediately. Pass additional cheese on the side.

*Trenette con Pesto, Patate, e Fagiolini (Trenette with Pesto, Potatoes, and Green Beans)*

# Of Saints and Pasta

March 19 dawned as a rainy and raw day. Salemi, a small town in the Belice valley in Sicily, was my destination, and I had come bringing a group of Americans with me who were anxious to see and be part of the festivities connected with the feast of St. Joseph and the *tavole di San Giuseppe,* the tables of St. Joseph. On this day, in many towns throughout Sicily, homage is paid to St. Joseph in a special way. The fact that the saint's feast day falls during Lent is no detriment to the offerings of food. Tables laden with hundreds of meatless dishes, including everything from *arancine* (rice balls) to *sfinge,* small puffs of pâte à choux, are served to family, friends, and strangers in thanksgiving for prayers answered, miracles worked, and intercessions pending, all in the name of St. Joseph, the carpenter. Salemi, however, is known for much more than the tables; it is also celebrated for the intricate breadwork ornaments that are handmade by the women of the town, who use as their tools common everyday items like combs, cheese graters, pastry wheels, table knives,

and sewing thimbles to fashion the ornaments that decorate the altars of St. Joseph. Just watching these women at work gives one a sense of their deep dedication to the feast and their immense sense of pride in being recognized as artisan bread sculptors who work for weeks in preparation for this day. To them, nothing is too good for St. Joseph.

A festive mood settles over Salemi as its citizens and busloads of visitors await the arrival of the priest who will bless the altars, after which the signal will be given that it is time to bring out the perciatelli, a thick spaghetti prepared by the townspeople.

It seems like an eternity as we stand and wait with the crush of people and marvel at the altars adorned with bread ornaments of stars, animals, flowers, and even St. Joseph's beard and staff. Oranges, with which Sicily is more than adequately blessed, are also part of the ornamentation and are striking combined with dark green ropes of laurel.

Finally the word begins to rumble through the crowd that it will only be a few more minutes before the perciatelli will be offered to anyone who wants it. The American group curiously wonders where the utensils and plates are. Suddenly a

rustle of noise is heard from one end of the town square and a huge, deep wooden trough at least 10 feet long is slowly shuffled by a small army of people through the throngs now gathered. Clouds of steam rise up from the trough and people begin to surge toward it. The incantation of the priest can barely be heard over the crowd, now with heads bowed in prayer. Everyone makes the sign of the cross. The American group, still puzzled as to what will happen next, looks around to see what the procedure is for serving but quickly dismisses this mind-set as people begin to use their hands to scoop up strands of pasta from the trough. We do the same and it is an unexpected and unique experience to taste spaghetti dressed only with olive oil, bread crumbs, and sugar. We walk away feeling privileged to have witnessed so ancient a ritual, and to have shared the food of complete strangers, and we are content to know that thanks to St. Joseph we would forever have a new reverence for a humble plate of pasta.

## MACCHERONI CON POLPETTINE DI MELANZANE

# Macaroni with Eggplant Meatballs

SERVES 6

*Here's a nice choice for an Italian-American vegetarian macaroni-and-"meatball" dish that my mother makes. The meatballs are made using cooked eggplant instead of ground meats. It is wonderfully surprising how good this tastes, and Mom always gets rave reviews. Any short cut of dried pasta such as macaroni, rigatoni, gemelli, or ziti would be a good choice.*

3 tablespoons olive oil

3 cloves garlic, minced

1 eggplant (about 12 ounces), peeled and diced

1 to 2 tablespoons water

1¼ cups fresh bread crumbs

½ cup minced fresh Italian parsley leaves

½ teaspoon fine sea salt

1½ teaspoons dried oregano

2 large eggs, slightly beaten

½ cup freshly grated Pecorino cheese

¼ cup vegetable oil

3 cups Tomato and Basil Sauce (page 52), kept hot

1 pound macaroni

Heat the olive oil in a large nonstick skillet or saucepan and slowly cook the garlic over medium heat until golden. Add the eggplant and 1 tablespoon of the water, cover, and steam the eggplant over low heat until very soft, about 10 minutes. Add the remaining water only if the eggplant begins to stick to the skillet. Stir the eggplant occasionally while it cooks. Set the eggplant aside and let it cool.

Combine the bread crumbs, parsley, salt, oregano, eggs, and cheese in a large bowl. Stir in the eggplant, mix well, and let it stand for 20 minutes. Scoop small amounts of the mixture into your hands and form meatballs the size of a small egg. There should be enough to make about eighteen.

Heat the vegetable oil in a large sauté pan over medium-high heat, then fry the meatballs, turning them occasionally so they brown evenly, or bake them in an oiled casserole dish in a preheated 350°F oven until browned, 20 to 25 minutes. Transfer the meatballs to the tomato sauce and keep hot.

Cook the macaroni according to the directions on page 29. Drain and place the macaroni in a serving dish. Mix with some of the tomato sauce, then arrange the meatballs and sauce on top of the pasta, and serve immediately. Pass additional cheese for sprinkling on top.

NOTE: *When forming the meatballs, wet your hands occasionally to prevent the mixture from sticking.*

## ORECCHIETTE CON RADICCHIELLA
# Little Ears with Dandelion Greens

SERVES 4 TO 6

Orecchiette, *little ears, is an endearing name given to pasta from Puglia, the region at Italy's heel. The semolina-flour-and-water dough is still made by hand in many locales where small pieces of dough are rolled against the tip of a butter knife to form the traditional shape. The classic accompaniment to orecchiette is* cima di rape, *a vibrant, bitter-tasting green, and the best I have ever eaten was at Ristorante Plaza in the beautiful city of Lecce. But Pugliese cooks concoct many combinations, include peppery arugula, chickpeas, and tomato sauce. In this recipe dandelion greens become a delicious partner to store-bought orecchiette. Orecchiette are a thicker pasta, so the cooking time will be longer than for thinner forms.*

⅓ cup plus 1 tablespoon extra virgin olive oil

¼ cup fresh bread crumbs

¼ cup freshly grated Pecorino Romano cheese

1½ pounds dandelion greens, washed well and stemmed

½ cup diced scallions

1 cup seeded and diced yellow bell pepper (one 8-ounce pepper)

1 small hot red or green pepper, seeded and diced, or 2 teaspoons dried red pepper flakes

3 cloves garlic, minced

Grinding of coarse black pepper

¼ to ½ teaspoon fine sea salt, to your taste

1 pound store-bought orecchiette

Heat 1 tablespoon of the olive oil in a large sauté pan over medium heat. Stir in the bread crumbs and "toast" the crumbs, stirring them in the oil until they are golden brown. Transfer them to a bowl and stir in the cheese. Set aside. Wipe out the sauté pan and set aside.

Bring a large pot of water to a boil, add the dandelion greens, and cook, uncovered, for 6 to 7 minutes. Drain in a colander; when cool, squeeze out as much water as possible, reserving ¼ cup. Transfer the greens to a cutting board and coarsely chop them. There should be about 1½ cups. Set aside.

Heat the remaining ⅓ cup of the olive oil in the sauté pan over medium heat. Stir in the scallions and yellow and hot peppers and cook until the scallions look translucent and glazed. Stir in the garlic and dandelion greens and cook for 2 to 3 minutes. Stir in the black pepper and salt and set aside off the heat.

Cook the orecchiette according to the directions on page 29 for store-bought pasta. These will take a little longer to cook because of their thickness, so test occasionally for doneness. Drain the pasta and transfer to the sauté pan along with the reserved greens water. Reheat the dandelion-and-orecchiette mixture, stirring quickly to combine everything well. Transfer the mixture to a serving platter. Sprinkle the bread-crumb-and-cheese mixture over the top and serve immediately.

NOTE: *This is a spicy dish; adjust the amount of salt and hot pepper to taste.*

*Orecchiette con Radicchiella (Little Ears with Dandelion Greens)*

ORECCHIETTE CON FELCI, GORGONZOLA, E NOCI

# Little Ears with Fiddleheads, Gorgonzola, and Walnuts

SERVES 4 TO 6

*Although orecchiette (little ears) are traditionally served with some type of bitter green such as cime di rape, I also like combining this interesting pasta shape with tender fiddlehead ferns. Fiddleheads appear in the grocery store for a short time in the spring. Although this recipe is a departure from the traditional Pugliese types, the addition of leeks, Gorgonzola cheese, and walnuts makes this dish a delight to make and enjoy as* cucina nuova *(new cooking).*

¾ pound fiddlehead ferns

4 cups water

1½ teaspoons sea salt

2 large leeks, green tops discarded and root ends trimmed

1 tablespoon butter

1 tablespoon extra virgin olive oil

¼ cup dry white wine

¼ pound Italian Gorgonzola cheese, cut into small pieces

Grinding of black pepper

1 pound orecchiette

½ cup chopped walnuts

Fill a bowl with cold water and soak the fiddleheads for a few minutes. Then drain them and set aside. Bring the 4 cups water to a boil in a medium-size saucepan. Add the fiddleheads and 1 teaspoon of the salt. Cook the fiddleheads, uncovered, just until the stems are tender, 5 to 8 minutes. Drain them in a colander and set aside.

Cut the leeks in half lengthwise, then wash them well under running water to remove any sand. Cut the leeks into slices and set aside. There should be about 2 cups.

In a sauté pan over medium heat, combine the butter and olive oil. When the butter is melted, add the leeks and cook them, stirring occasionally, until they begin to soften. Add the fiddleheads and cook for 3 to 4 minutes, stirring occasionally. Increase the heat to high and pour in the wine. Allow the wine to evaporate. Reduce the heat to medium-low, add the cheese, and stir until it melts. Stir in the remaining ½ teaspoon salt and the pepper. Keep the sauce warm while the orecchiette are cooking.

Cook the orecchiette according to the directions on page 29. Drain them, reserving 2 tablespoons of the cooking water. Return the orecchiette to the pot with the water. Stir in the fiddlehead mixture over low heat, combining the mixture well.

Transfer the orecchiette and fiddlehead sauce to a platter and sprinkle the nuts over the top. Serve immediately.

TAGLIATELLE VERDI AL RADICCHIO ED ASIAGO

# Green Ribbon Noodles with Radicchio and Asiago Cheese

SERVES 4 TO 6

*Tagliatelle is similar to fettucine, ribbons of handmade or store-bought pasta about ¼ inch wide. It is said that they were first made for Lucretia Borgia to commemorate her marriage to the Duke of Este in 1487. Lucretia's long blond tresses were said to inspire the creation of tagliatelle.*

*In this adaptation spinach-flavored tagliatelle is paired with a sauce of slightly bitter-tasting ruby-red radicchio, one of many types of chicory.*

½ cup extra virgin olive oil

2 large shallots, minced

1 pound radicchio, washed and thinly sliced

6 tablespoons dry white wine

Fine sea salt to taste

1 pound Tagliatelle Verdi (page 20)

1 cup freshly grated Asiago or Parmigiano-Reggiano cheese

Heat the olive oil in a large sauté pan, then cook the shallots over medium heat, stirring, until softened. Add the radicchio and cook, stirring, for 2 to 3 minutes. The color will turn from red to rust. Add the wine and salt, cover the pan, and simmer the ingredients for 5 minutes. Keep the sauce warm and set aside.

Cook the tagliatelle following the directions on page 30.

Drain the pasta, reserving 2 tablespoons of the cooking water. Stir the pasta and the water into the sauce, then stir in half the cheese. Transfer the mixture to a serving platter, sprinkle the top with the remaining ½ cup cheese, and serve immediately.

*Penne ai Pistacci, Asparagi,
e Panna (Penne with
Pistachios, Asparagus, and
Cream)*

PENNE AI PISTACCI, ASPARAGI, E PANNA

# Penne with Pistachios, Asparagus, and Cream

SERVES 4 TO 6

*Perugia is a city of learning with its universities and the regional center of Umbria. One reaches it by winding one's way up a hilltop where a breathtaking view of the Tiber valley awaits. The Etruscan, medieval, Renaissance, and modern elements of the city all meld together to create a fascinating history of architecture. The food is fascinating, too. This is black truffle and spit-roasted porchetta (pork) country, and when it comes to pasta, the Umbrians combine it with what nature provides: an abundance of wild fennel and wild asparagus. This dish made by master teacher Mario Ragni is one of my favorites.*

⅓ cup whole shelled natural pistachio nuts

2 cups water

2 teaspoons fine sea salt

1 pound thin asparagus, washed, woody ends removed, and stalks cut into thirds

¼ cup (½ stick) unsalted butter

1 large clove garlic, peeled and cut in half lengthwise

¼ teaspoon ground white pepper

⅓ cup dry white wine

1 cup half and half

¼ cup heavy cream

1 pound penne

½ cup freshly grated Parmigiano-Reggiano cheese

Preheat the oven to 350°F.

Spread the nuts on an aluminum pie plate and toast them in the oven for 5 to 7 minutes, watching carefully so they do not burn. Transfer the nuts to a cutting board, mince them, and set aside.

Bring the water to a boil in a pot. Add ½ teaspoon of the salt and the asparagus. Cook, uncovered, over medium-high heat just until a knife tip is easily inserted into the asparagus, about 3 minutes. Drain and set aside.

In a sauté pan, melt the butter over medium heat. Add the garlic and press on it with a wooden spoon to release its flavor. When the garlic starts to brown around the edges, remove and discard it. Add the asparagus and white pepper, raise the heat to high, and pour in the wine. Stir the mixture carefully for about 1 minute. Reduce the heat to medium. Mix the half and half and heavy cream together and pour it over the asparagus mixture. Cook for 2 minutes; the sauce should be thick and velvety like heavy cream. Stir in the remaining 1½ teaspoons salt. Keep the mixture warm while the penne cooks.

Cook the penne according to the directions on page 29. Drain and return to the cooking pot. Pour the asparagus sauce over the penne and stir carefully over low heat. Add the cheese and continue to stir until the cheese melts. Transfer the penne to a serving platter, sprinkle the nuts over the top, and serve immediately.

PENNETTE CON VERDURE

# Pennette with Vegetables

SERVES 4 TO 6

*In this vibrant-looking and light-tasting dish, pennette, tiny slant-cut pasta, the cousin of penne, are the perfect match for diced vegetables. An added bonus is that this can be considered a low-fat meal, since the olive oil, milk, and cheese are used sparingly. It is best to eat this dish with a spoon, which also makes it especially appealing to small children.*

1 tablespoon extra virgin olive oil

1 medium-size onion, minced

2 cloves garlic, minced

2 medium-size carrots, minced

1½ cups diced butternut squash (½ pound squash)

Fine sea salt to taste

Freshly ground black pepper to taste

2 tablespoons water

1½ cups fresh or thawed frozen petite peas

¾ pound #42 pennette

½ cup hot low-fat milk

½ cup freshly grated Parmigiano-Reggiano cheese

¼ cup julienned fresh basil leaves

Heat the olive oil in a large sauté pan, then slowly cook the onion and garlic over medium heat just until they soften. Add the carrots, squash, salt and pepper to taste, and the water. Cover the pan and cook until the squash is just tender, about 10 minutes. Add the peas during the last 2 minutes of cooking. Correct the seasoning and set aside.

Meanwhile cook the pennette until *al dente* as directed on page 29. Drain the pasta and add it imme-diately to the sauté pan with the vegetables. Stir in the hot milk and ¼ cup of the cheese and heat just until all the ingredients are hot.

Transfer the pennette mixture to a large platter. Mix in the basil and sprinkle on the remaining ¼ cup cheese. Serve immediately.

# Rigatoni con Salsa Caprese

SERVES 6 TO 8

*Rigatoni teams nicely with this easy sauce I call* salsa caprese *because it uses the very ingredients that make up the more popular* insalata caprese, *a salad of fresh creamy mozzarella cheese, pungent and peppery basil leaves, and fresh plum tomatoes popular on the isle of Capri. In a pinch, canned plum tomatoes can be used.*

3 tablespoons extra virgin olive oil

1 medium-size onion, diced

1 large clove garlic, minced

4 cups diced plum tomatoes

2 teaspoons fine sea salt

Grinding of fresh black pepper

⅓ cup dry red wine

2 tablespoons sugar

½ cup fresh basil leaves, shredded

1 pound store-bought rigatoni

One 8-ounce ball fresh mozzarella cheese, diced

1 cup finely chopped well-drained cooked spinach

Heat the olive oil over medium heat in a 4-quart saucepan. Cook the onion, stirring, until it becomes soft, then add the garlic and cook, stirring, until the garlic is soft but still white. Stir in the tomatoes, salt, pepper, wine, and sugar. Reduce the heat to a simmer, cover the pot, and cook the sauce for 20 minutes. The sauce should still be loose, but not thin. Stir in the basil leaves. Set the sauce aside and keep warm.

Meanwhile, cook the rigatoni according to the instructions on page 29. When *al dente*, drain the riga-toni, reserving 2 tablespoons of the cooking water. Return the rigatoni to the pot and, over low heat, stir in the reserved water, 1 cup of the tomato sauce, the cheese, and spinach. Stir until the cheese melts.

Transfer the mixture to a shallow platter. Serve at once, passing additional sauce on the side. Save the remaining tomato sauce for other uses such as on pizza or in stews. Or freeze it for future use.

*Maltagliati di Bietole Gialle
Con Verdure Arrostite (Badly
Cut Yellow Beet Pasta with
Roasted Vegetables)*

MALTAGLIATI DI BIETOLE GIALLE CON VERDURE ARROSTITE

# Badly Cut Yellow Beet Pasta with Roasted Vegetables

SERVES 6 USING 6 DOZEN MALTAGLIATI

*Maltagliati means badly cut, referring to randomly cut triangular pieces of dough, which are added to soups. This conjures up visions of rustic charm but when I make them, I give them an element of elegance by adding pureed yellow beets to the dough, resulting in sunny, golden-hued pasta. The more common red beet can be substituted if yellow ones are not available. The sauce, a combination of roasted carrots and shallots, adds texture and a slight sweet taste, while the beet tops, cooked along with the maltagliati, balance the sweetness with their sharpness and lend a wonderful color contrast. Save time by making the maltagliati ahead and drying them.*

FOR THE PASTA
*(makes at least 24 dozen)*

1 small yellow or red beet

4 large eggs

3 cups unbleached all-purpose flour

½ cup finely ground durum semolina flour

2 teaspoons salt

FOR THE SAUCE

2 teaspoons extra virgin olive oil

5 medium-size carrots (12 ounces), cut into
¼-inch-thick rounds

2 large shallots, peeled

Fine sea salt to taste

Grated zest of 1 large lemon

5 tablespoons butter

TO COOK THE PASTA

6 quarts water

1 tablespoon salt

6 dozen maltagliati

Green tops from 6 medium-size beets,
stemmed, washed well, and torn into pieces

TO FINISH

¼ cup freshly grated Parmigiano-Reggiano
cheese

Preheat the oven to 350°F. Remove the top from the beet, leaving 2 inches of stem attached. Reserve the top. Cut the beet in half lengthwise and wrap the halves in aluminum foil. Bake until a knife easily pierces the flesh, about 30 minutes.

Alternately, wrap the beet halves tightly in plastic wrap and microwave on high power for 5 minutes. Or

boil the beet for 20 to 25 minutes. When cool, peel and discard the skin. Puree the beet in a food processor or blender. You will need 2 tablespoons of pureed beet.

If making the dough in a processor, add the eggs to the pureed beet and pulse to blend. Mix 2 cups of the unbleached flour with the semolina flour and salt and add to the bowl of the processor. Process until the

*continued*

mixture begins to form in a ball. Add only enough of the remaining flour until the dough holds together as one piece and cleans the sides of the bowl. Remove the dough from the processor and knead it on a lightly floured work surface for 2 to 3 minutes. Let the dough rest under a bowl for 30 minutes to relax the gluten and make it easier to roll.

To make the dough by hand, mix together 2 cups of the unbleached flour, the semolina flour, and salt directly on the work surface. Fashion a well in the center. Crack the eggs in the center of the well and beat the eggs with a fork until foamy. Add the pureed beet and mix well. Take care not to break the wall of flour. With your hands, bring the flour from the inside of the wall into the egg mixture. Work in a clockwise fashion. Form a ball of dough using the remaining flour as needed. Push the excess flour aside and knead the dough until it is smooth and soft but not sticky, about 5 minutes. Let the dough rest under a bowl for 30 minutes.

Cut the dough into four equal pieces. Work with one piece at a time and keep the rest covered. With a rolling pin, roll the dough out into a 9 × 6-inch rectangle. Flour the piece lightly. Using a pasta machine, flatten the dough to the last setting following the directions on page 11. Trim the sheet of dough to 36 × 5½ inches. Keep the trimmings to re-roll later.

Cut the sheet in half crosswise into two 18-inch-long pieces. Cut each half lengthwise down the middle to form two strips. Cut nine 2 × 2¾-inch pieces from each strip, then cut the pieces diagonally to form triangles. These are the maltagliati.

Cover several cookie sheets with clean kitchen towels and arrange the maltagliati on them in single layers. Repeat the process with the remaining pieces of dough, separating the layers of maltagliati with more kitchen towels.

*Cutting the maltagliati*

To make the maltagliati ahead, allow them to dry thoroughly on the towels for at least 2 days. This may take even longer if it is humid. The maltagliati are sufficiently dried when the edges begin to curl and they feel brittle. Store them in airtight containers for up to 2 months.

Preheat the oven to 350°F. Brush a cookie sheet with the olive oil and arrange the sliced carrots in a single layer on the sheet. Cut the shallots into halves and place them on the sheet. Roast until a knife easily pierces the vegetables, about 30 minutes. Turn the vegetables once halfway through the cooking time.

Transfer the carrots to a bowl. Cut the shallots into small pieces and add to the carrots. Toss with the salt and lemon zest.

Heat the butter in a large sauté pan while the pasta cooks.

Bring the water to a boil in a pasta pot, add the salt, 6 dozen of the maltagliati, and the torn beet tops. Cook until the maltagliati are *al dente*, about 4 minutes.

Drain the pasta and beet tops, leaving a little water clinging to the pasta. Transfer the mixture to the sauté pan, add the carrots and shallots, and mix together quickly over medium-high heat until hot. Transfer the maltagliati mixture to a platter, sprinkle with the cheese, and serve immediately.

NOTE: *To sauce all the maltagliati, quadruple the sauce ingredients.*

SPAGHETTI CON SALSA DI POMODORO E PORRO ARROSTITO

# Spaghetti with Roasted Tomato and Leek Sauce

SERVES 4 TO 6

*Salsa di Pomodoro e Porro Arrostito, whether it is the smooth or chunky version on page 57, can stand alone with any cooked pasta but the smooth version really shines when combined with Sardinian feta cheese and sugar snap peas. With the sauce on hand, dinner is on the table in the time it takes to boil the pasta. If Sardinian feta cheese is not available, substitute Greek feta cheese.*

4 to 6 quarts water

1 pound store-bought spaghetti

1 tablespoon fine sea salt

½ pound sugar snap peas, rinsed and drained

1 recipe Roasted Tomato and Leek Sauce (page 57)

½ pound Sardinian feta cheese, coarsely crumbled

Coarsely ground black pepper to taste

Bring 4 to 6 quarts of water to a rolling boil in a pasta pot. Add the spaghetti and salt and stir with a pasta fork to separate the spaghetti and submerge the strands under the water. Cover the pot, bring the water back to a boil, remove the cover, and cook until the spaghetti is almost al dente. Add the sugar snap peas to the pot and continue to cook until the spaghetti is ready. Drain the spaghetti and peas in a colander. Reserve 1 tablespoon of the cooking water.

Return the spaghetti and sugar snap peas to the pot. Stir in the sauce and reserved cooking water over low heat. Stir in half the cheese and, when the mixture is heated through, transfer it to a shallow platter. Sprinkle the remaining cheese over the top, give it a grinding of black pepper, and serve immediately.

FRITTELLE DI TAGLIERINI
# Fried Pasta Wedges

SERVES 4

*Frittelle usually means small pieces of batter-fried foods. Here it means crunchy fried wedges of thin taglierini (similar to angel hair) that are held together in a cream-and-vegetable sauce. The nice thing about this recipe is that the taste and texture can easily change with what's in the refrigerator. Small pieces of cooked vegetables such as artichoke hearts or asparagus are delicious additions, as are a handful of fresh herbs. For a nice change of pace, serve* frittelle *as a Sunday night supper and you will be surprised at how good it can taste as a leftover. To save time, assemble the entire dish up to the point of coating the* frittelle *in egg and bread crumbs and refrigerate it.*

2 tablespoons butter

2 tablespoons unbleached all-purpose flour

1 cup hot milk

½ teaspoon fine sea salt

¼ teaspoon celery salt

Grated zest of 1 large lemon

4 large eggs

2 tablespoons freshly grated Parmigiano-Reggiano cheese

1 cup diced cooked vegetables such as green beans, asparagus, or artichoke hearts, or a combination of vegetables

½ pound fresh or store-bought taglierini or angel hair pasta

1½ to 2 cups Toasted Bread Crumbs (page 89)

½ cup vegetable oil for frying

Melt the butter in a 1-quart saucepan over medium heat. Gradually whisk in the flour and cook for 1 minute. Slowly whisk in the hot milk, then cook the mixture, stirring with a wooden spoon until the sauce thickens and coats the spoon, about 4 minutes. Stir in the salts and zest, remove from the heat, and quickly whisk in two of the eggs, one at a time. Stir in the cheese. Pour the sauce into a large bowl, stir in the vegetables and press a sheet of buttered wax paper onto the surface of the sauce to keep a skin from forming and set aside.

Cook the taglierini according to the directions on page 29. Drain well and add to the sauce, mixing thor-oughly to coat the pasta well. Turn the mixture out onto a lightly oiled cookie sheet or marble board. Shape the mixture into an even-looking round, about 10 inches in diameter and 1 inch high. Cover with plastic wrap and refrigerate for 1 hour. This will make it easier to cut into wedges before frying.

Beat the remaining 2 eggs in a shallow, wide bowl. Mound the bread crumbs on a sheet of wax paper and season them with a little salt.

With a sharp knife, cut the round into quarters; cut each quarter into two wedges. Dip each wedge into the egg, evenly coating it, then coat it in bread crumbs and set aside on a cookie sheet.

Heat the vegetable oil in a heavy-duty skillet over medium-high heat. Fry the wedges on both sides until the coating is crisp and browned. Add additional oil if the pan seems too dry. Remove the wedges with a slotted spatula and let them drain on brown paper. Serve warm.

NOTE: *These are also good topped with a little tomato sauce.*

PANE GRATTUGIATO

## Toasted Bread Crumbs

MAKES 2 CUPS

*Here is a simple recipe for making toasted bread crumbs. Use it whenever a recipe calls for them. Toasted crumbs can be made only from good quality bread that is somewhat coarse in texture. The recipe can be doubled or tripled as needed.*

¼ cup extra virgin olive oil

3 tablespoons unsalted butter

2 cups bread crumbs

Fine sea salt to taste

In a medium-size skillet, heat the oil and butter together until the butter melts. Stir to blend the mixture well over medium heat. Add the bread crumbs and stir constantly with a wooden spoon until the crumbs absorb all of the oil-and-butter mixture and are golden brown. Season with the salt and remove the crumbs to a bowl to cool. When cool, transfer the crumbs to an airtight container and store in the refrigerator. They will keep for several weeks.

*Mezza Mezza Frittata di Pasta (Half and Half Pasta Omelet)*

MEZZA MEZZA FRITTATA DI PASTA
# Half and Half Pasta Omelet

SERVES 10

*A few olives, a handful of herbs, some chips of cheese, and last night's leftover pasta—these are the things from which, in days gone by, frugal Italian cooks created a frittata, an omelet. In this version, plain fettucine and spinach-flavored fettucine are combined with grated vegetables and cooked side by side in a large sauté pan for a really gourmet look. Although this dish is delicious made with commercially prepared fettucine, it is much lighter-tasting if made with homemade. Capellini (angel hair pasta) is also a good choice. Can't have eggs? See the note at the end of the recipe about substituting Egg Beaters, low-fat cheese, and store-bought fettucine.*

6 large eggs

1 teaspoon plus 1 tablespoon fine sea salt

Grinding of black pepper

1½ cups (6 ounces) grated zucchini

1 medium-size carrot, grated

1½ cups (6 ounces) cubed Italian Fontina cheese

⅛ teaspoon freshly grated nutmeg

3 tablespoons minced fresh mint leaves

3 quarts water

6 ounces plain fettucine, homemade (page 9) or store-bought

6 ounces spinach fettucine, homemade (page 20) or store-bought

¼ cup extra virgin olive oil

2 tablespoons butter

Crack three of the eggs into each of two large bowls. Stir ½ teaspoon of the salt, and a grinding of black pepper into each bowl.

Stir the zucchini into one bowl and the carrot into the other. Divide equally and stir the cheese into each bowl. Stir the nutmeg into the carrot mixture and the mint into the zucchini mixture. Set the bowls aside.

In a pasta pot with an insert bring the water to a boil. Add the 1 tablespoon of salt and the plain fettucine. Cook for only 2 to 3 minutes for fresh or follow the directions on page 29 for commercially prepared, being careful to cook the fettucine *al dente*. With a pasta scoop, drain the fettucine from the water,

shaking off the excess and transfer it to the bowl with the zucchini mixture. Toss the ingredients gently together and set aside.

In the same pot, cook the spinach fettucine until *al dente* and drain with a pasta scoop, shaking off the excess water. Transfer the fettucine to the bowl with the carrot mixture and toss well. Set aside.

In a large (12-inch) nonstick sauté pan, heat together 2 tablespoons of the olive oil and 1 tablespoon of the butter. Make sure the oil and butter evenly coat the bottom of the pan. Transfer the plain fettucine mixture to one half of the pan, smoothing out the top so it is even. Pour the spinach fettucine

*continued*

mixture in the other half of the pan next to the plain fettucine and smooth the top. Make sure the two types of fettucine meet in the center of the pan. Cook over medium heat until the frittata easily moves away from the sides of the pan and moves freely when the pan is shaken.

Place a serving dish, pizza pan, or rimless baking sheet larger than the diameter of the sauté pan over the top and carefully invert the frittata onto the dish or pan. Set aside. Return the sauté pan to the heat. Add the remaining 2 tablespoons olive oil and 1 tablespoon butter and when it is hot, slide the under-cooked side of the frittata back into the pan and cook the other side.

Invert the frittata once it is cooked onto a serving dish. Let cool slightly, then cut into wedges to serve.

TIP: Use a lightweight well-seasoned nonstick sauté pan for best results. The frittata will be easier to invert and less likely to stick to the pan.

NOTE: *To make a low-fat, low-cholesterol version of this frittata, substitute commercially prepared fettucine, Egg Beaters (using 10 ounces for the 6 eggs), and low-fat cheese.*

# Pasta with Meat

orzo • pappardelle • penne • quadrucci • ravioli • rotelle • rigatoni • spaghetti • tortellini • trenette • z

## MACCHERONI ALLA CHITARRA

# Macaroni Made on the Guitar

SERVES 4 TO 6

*One of my treasured pasta-making implements is the handmade wooden* chitarra *that belonged to my grandmother, Maria Assunta Saporito. The* chitarra *is a rectangular form strung with taut, thin wire strings that is used for cutting the classic Abruzzese pasta known as* maccheroni alla chitarra, *which is a little thicker cut of spaghetti. Chitarra means guitar and the implement is so called because as pasta sheets are rolled over it, the wires produce melodic sounds. The appropriate sauce to use with this pasta is a lamb ragù made with both sweet and hot peppers, which can be made several days ahead to save time. Two cups of sauce is enough to dress one recipe of the pasta. Freeze the remaining sauce for future use.*

*The* chitarra *is also handy for making* quadrucci, *tiny squares of pasta used for soup (see opposite for a photo of the technique used to make them).*

FOR THE SAUCE *(makes 4 cups)*

3 cloves garlic, peeled and cut in half

2 tablespoons fresh rosemary leaves

2 tablespoons fresh thyme leaves

⅓ cup extra virgin olive oil

1 small hot red pepper, seeded and cut into thin strips

2 medium-size red bell peppers, seeded and cut into thin strips

1 bay leaf

1 pound ground lamb

⅔ cup dry red wine

1 pound fresh plum tomatoes, seeded and chopped

1 teaspoon fine sea salt

Freshly ground black pepper to taste

FOR THE PASTA AND TO FINISH

1 recipe Handmade Pasta dough (page 9) or 1 pound store-bought spaghetti

Freshly grated Pecorino cheese for sprinkling

To make the sauce, mince the garlic, rosemary, and thyme together and set aside. Heat the olive oil in a medium-size sauté pan, add the minced mixture, and cook over medium heat until it begins to soften. Add the peppers and bay leaf and continue to cook for about 1 minute. Add the lamb, browning it slowly over medium heat. Raise the heat to medium-high, add the wine, and stir with a wooden spoon until most of the wine has evaporated. Stir in the tomatoes, salt, and pepper and mix well. Cover the pan, reduce the heat to low, and simmer the sauce for 30 minutes, removing the cover during the last 10 minutes of cooking. Discard the bay leaf before using the sauce. Remove 2 cups of the sauce, cool, and store for future use. Keep the rest of the sauce warm while the maccheroni is cooking.

Divide the dough into six pieces.

If you have a *chitarra*, roll each piece of dough out on a lightly floured work surface until it is one third shorter than the length of the *chitarra*. Place the sheet of dough on top of the *chitarra* and roll over it forcefully with a rolling pin. The maccheroni will fall beneath the *chitarra*. Place the maccheroni on clean kitchen towels and continue with the rest of the dough. Alternately, thin the dough using a hand-crank pasta machine following the directions on page 11, then place it over the *chitarra* and roll over it with a rolling pin. If you do not have a *chitarra*, cut the pasta using a hand-crank pasta machine or by hand following the directions on page 14.

Cook the maccheroni according to the directions on page 30 for fresh pasta or page 29 for store-brought pasta until it is *al dente*, 3 to 4 minutes. Drain the maccheroni, reserving 2 tablespoons of the cooking water. Return the *maccheroni* to the pot, add the sauce and the reserved cooking water, and stir well. Transfer the mixture to a serving platter. Serve immediately and pass the cheese for sprinkling on top.

NOTE: *To purchase a* chittara, *see the mail-order section, page 160.*

*Rolling and cutting a thinned strip of dough into spaghetti on the* chitarra.

*Cutting spaghetti crosswise to form quadrucci.*

PETTOLE CON SALSA DI AGNELLO E VINO DI SCIAMPAGNA

# Pettole with Lamb and Champagne Sauce

SERVES 4 TO 6

*Caserta, one of the provinces of the region of Campania, is home to my friend Mario Cipolla, a charming and engaging man who now helps his son, Mauro, run Caffè d'Arte, an espresso bar in Seattle. Mario's grandmother Maria Grazia was a clever cook who used her wits to provide delicious meals. One of Mario's favorite dishes from his grandmother's kitchen is a country-style pasta called pettole, for which there is a charming tale that goes like this: Beatrice, a beautiful peasant girl, went to a dance and saw and flirted with a noble-looking soldier, who asked for a turn on the dance floor. The soldier whispered in her ear: "Beatrice, everyone says that you are a good cook, can you make me something wonderful to eat?" So Beatrice invited him to her cottage, poor as it was, and scrubbed and cleaned all day in anticipation of his visit. Then she began making dough from water, flour, and a drop of olive oil. The soldier arrived carrying a bottle of expensive champagne and asked her what she was making to go with it. "Pettole," she answered. The soldier, realizing as he looked around that he was in humble surroundings, suggested that she add some champagne to the dough but she declined and added it instead to the meager lamb sauce she had made and in that instant elevated pettole into a dish fit for her noble soldier. And, according to Mario, that is how pettole with a lamb and champagne sauce came to be the most asked for dish from his grandmother. For this delicious adaptation, the sauce is thickened with half and half. Use the recipe for Pici #1 or #2 on page 18 to make the dough, but cut the dough like pappardelle, following the directions on page 21, or use store-bought pappardelle.*

2 tablespoons extra virgin olive oil

1 large clove garlic, minced

1 pound lamb stew meat, trimmed of fat and cut into bite-size pieces

1 cup dry champagne

1 cup hot homemade Veal Stock (page 46) or beef broth (page 45)

5 fresh or canned plum tomatoes, peeled, seeded, and coarsely chopped

1½ teaspoons fine sea salt

¼ teaspoon coarsely ground black pepper

2 tablespoons unbleached all-purpose flour

¼ cup half and half

8 fresh basil leaves, torn into small pieces

1 pound homemade pettole or store-bought pappardelle

*Pettole con Salsa di Agnello e Vino di Sciampagna (Pettole with Lamb and Champagne Sauce)*

*continued*

In a medium-size sauté pan over medium-high heat, heat the olive oil, then add the garlic and cook, stirring, until it softens. Add the lamb pieces and brown them. Pour in ½ cup of the champagne, stir the mixture well for about 4 minutes, and allow the foam to subside. Reduce the heat to a simmer and stir in the stock, tomatoes, salt, and pepper. Cover the pan and let the sauce simmer until the meat is tender, 45 to 55 minutes.

Drain the meat in a mesh strainer set over a bowl to catch the liquid. Set the meat aside in a separate bowl. Return all but ¼ cup of the liquid to the pan (there should be 2 cups of liquid) and stir in the remaining ½ cup champagne. Cook, uncovered, over low heat until the mixture begins to simmer.

Whisk the flour into the reserved ¼ cup liquid, then whisk it into the simmering sauce and cook until the mixture begins to thicken. Whisk in the half and half and continue to cook for 2 minutes. Turn off the heat, return the lamb to the pan, and stir in the basil. Cover the sauce and keep warm while the pettole are cooking.

Cook the pettole according to the directions on page 30. Drain them, reserving 2 tablespoons of the water, and return them to the pasta pot. Stir in the sauce and the reserved cooking water. Mix carefully, transfer the mixture to a deep platter, and serve immediately.

## Variation

This dish is equally as delicious with veal shoulder, trimmed from the bone and cut into pieces.

NOTE: *For even browning of the meat, wipe the pieces with paper towels so they are as dry as possible.*

NOTE: *Save the veal shoulder bones to make Veal Stock (page 46).*

RIGATONI E BROCCOLI SICILIANI

# Sicilian Rigatoni and Cauliflower Casserole

SERVES 16

*In Palermo, Sicily, cauliflower is called* broccolo, *while in the rest of Italy it is called* cavolfiore *and is a favorite vegetable for marinated salads, batter-fried, and, most popular of all, combined with macaroni. The original recipe for this rigatoni-and-cauliflower casserole belonged to Sicilian cook Lucia Pullo Priolisi, whose daughter Marie passed it on to me. I have made some cooking step changes, preferring to bake the meatballs instead of frying them and roasting the cauliflower at the same time. This dish is a perfect choice for a crowd because it will easily serve up to sixteen people, and can be made ahead of time and reheated. Any short-cut pasta can be used but because the pasta will be baked after it is boiled, it should be firmer than usual when drained.*

¼ cup extra virgin olive oil

Olive oil cooking spray

1 large head cauliflower (2 pounds), washed and trimmed into 1-inch florets

½ cup fresh bread crumbs

5 tablespoons milk

1 pound lean ground beef

1 teaspoon dried oregano

½ teaspoon salt

¼ teaspoon coarsely ground black pepper

¾ cup freshly grated Pecorino cheese

1 medium-size onion, coarsely chopped

2 cloves garlic, minced

4 cups prepared tomato sauce of your choice

1 pound rigatoni or other short type of macaroni

Coat the bottom of one 13½ × 9-inch baking dish with 2 tablespoons of the olive oil and set aside.

Lightly coat another 13½ × 9-inch baking dish and one cookie sheet with olive oil spray and set aside.

Preheat the oven to 350°F.

Dry the cauliflower florets with a kitchen towel and transfer them to the olive-oil-coated baking dish. Toss them with a spoon to evenly coat them with the oil. Set aside.

In a large bowl, combine the bread crumbs with the milk and let the mixture stand for a couple of minutes.

Add the beef, oregano, salt, pepper, and ¼ cup of the cheese. Mix to combine the ingredients, then, with wet hands, form 1-inch meatballs and place them on the cookie sheet.

Bake the meatballs and the cauliflower at the same time, removing the meatballs after 30 minutes and the florets after 40 minutes. During the cooking time, stir the florets a couple of times. They should be cooked but hold their shape and be slightly browned.

Heat the remaining 2 tablespoons olive oil in a medium-size saucepan over medium heat and cook

*continued*

the onion, stirring, until it softens; add the garlic and cook until the garlic softens. Stir in the tomato sauce and heat until hot. Set aside.

Meanwhile, cook the rigatoni according to the instructions on page 29, until they are still somewhat firm but not raw. Drain the rigatoni and transfer them to a large bowl.

Mix the rigatoni with 1 cup of the tomato sauce. Add the cauliflower and another cup of the tomato

sauce and mix well. Add the meatballs and another cup of the tomato sauce and mix again.

Divide and transfer half of the mixture to each of the baking dishes. Spread half of the remaining cup tomato sauce over each dish. Sprinkle the top of each dish with half of the remaining ½ cup cheese.

Cover each dish with a sheet of aluminum foil. Bake, covered, for 20 minutes. Uncover and bake 5 minutes more. Serve immediately.

## RIGATONI CON SALSA DI CIPOLLA
# Rigatoni with Onion Sauce

SERVES 4 TO 6

*This delicious onion sauce was served to me by my friend Mario Rogni, who lives in Perugia in the region of Umbria. What made the sauce so memorable was Mario's homemade lard, but I have substituted salt pork with good results. Use a rigatoni or ziti cut of pasta for this dish, which is cooked ahead of time, then added to the sauce and cooked briefly again as the sauce thickens.*

1 pound rigatoni or other short-cut pasta
1 tablespoon unsalted butter, softened
¼ pound lean salt pork, finely diced
1 large onion, peeled and thinly sliced
1 tablespoon unbleached all-purpose flour

1 to 1½ cups hot homemade (page 45) or canned low-sodium beef broth
¼ cup plus 2 tablespoons freshly grated Parmigiano-Reggiano cheese
2 teaspoons coarsely ground black pepper

In a pasta pot with an insert, cook the rigatoni until it is *al dente*, according to the directions on page 29. Drain the rigatoni, transfer to a bowl, and coat them with the butter. Set aside.

In a large sauté pan over medium heat, cook the salt pork and onion together until the salt pork is browned

and has rendered its fat. Sprinkle the flour over the salt pork and onion and stir to blend. Stir in the rigatoni. Pour in half of the beef stock, stirring. Add the cheese and remaining stock, stirring well. Remove from the heat, stir in the pepper, transfer the rigatoni and sauce to a pasta platter or bowl, and serve at once.

MALLOREDDUS A LA CAMPIDANESE

# Country-Style Sardinian Gnocchi with Sausage Sauce

SERVES 4 TO 6

*Malloreddus is the national pasta dish of Sardinia and the big cousin to fregola (page 113), another traditional pasta. The term* malloreddu *comes from the Latin* mallolus *and means morsel or little bits of pasta dough that are hand-rolled on a round reed basket to make the characteristic shape and lines in the dough. Another more recognizable word for this type of pasta is gnocchi, a little dumpling of flour and water. Malloreddus is made from* grano duro *(hard wheat flour) and there are many variations. They can be found in Italian specialty stores or ordered by mail (page 160). Here they are combined with saffron and tomato and served with fresh or store-bought Italian sausage flavored with fennel seeds. This recipe is from my Sardinian friends Mario and Giulia Cocco.*

1 teaspoon olive oil

¾ pound fresh (page 103) or store-bought Italian sausage with fennel seeds, casings removed and crumbled into pieces

3 cloves garlic, minced

1 to 2 teaspoons crushed fennel seeds, to your taste

1¾ pounds fresh tomatoes, peeled and coarsely chopped, or one 28-ounce can tomatoes

½ cup (2 ounces) diced drained Dried Tomatoes in Olive Oil (page 56)

1 tablespoon tomato paste

1 teaspoon fine sea salt

1 package powdered saffron dissolved in 2 tablespoons warm water

1 large bay leaf

6 fresh basil leaves, cut into thin strips

¾ pound plain or flavored malloreddus

½ cup grated Pecorino cheese

In a nonstick skillet, heat the olive oil, then add the sausage and cook slowly over medium heat until the meat is no longer pink but not browned. With a slotted spoon transfer the sausage to a bowl, leaving the fat behind.

Discard all but 1 teaspoon of the fat in the skillet. Add the garlic and fennel seeds and cook, stirring, until the garlic begins to turn golden brown. Stir in the fresh or canned tomatoes, dried tomatoes, tomato paste, salt, saffron, bay leaf, and basil leaves. Reduce the heat to medium-low and simmer the sauce, covered, for 10 minutes, stirring occasionally. Uncover the skillet and cook 5 minutes more. Return the sausage to the skillet, mixing it in well and cook 3 to 4 minutes longer. Cover the sauce and keep it warm while the malloreddus are cooking.

*continued*

Cook the malloreddus according to the directions on page 29 until *al dente*. Drain and transfer them to a large bowl. Remove the bay leaf from the sauce before adding it to the malloreddus. Pour 2¼ cups of the sauce (freeze the rest) over the malloreddus, mix well, then transfer the mixture to a serving platter. Sprinkle the cheese over the top and serve immediately.

NOTE: *Crush fennel seeds in a spice mill or on a cutting board with a chef's knife. To prevent the seeds from scattering off the board, spray the board with a little olive oil spray; the seeds will stay in place.*

*Malloreddus la Campidanese (Country-Style Sardinian Gnocchi with Sausage Sauce) (page 101)*

SALSICCIA FRESCA
## Fresh Italian Sausage

MAKES 5 POUNDS

*People are very surprised when they learn that making fresh Italian sausage does not necessarily mean investing in a fancy sausage machine. In fact, it takes less time to make it by hand than in a machine, which has to be cleaned and sterilized. A small, stainless steel hand sausage funnel, freshly ground pork butt, some seasonings, and natural hog casings are all you need. Before you fill the casing, determine if the sausage is mild or hot enough for your taste by cooking a small amount in a frying pan. Fresh Italian sausage can be made ahead and frozen for several months. Use it in recipes such as the malloreddus on page 101.*

5 pounds boneless pork butt with some fat, ground once on coarse grind and once on medium grind

2½ tablespoons coarse salt, or more to taste

2 tablespoons coarsely ground black pepper, or more to taste

3 to 4 tablespoons fennel seeds, to your taste

1 tablespoon dried red pepper flakes, or more to taste

1 package natural hog casings (available in grocery-store meat departments)

In a large bowl, combine the pork and all the seasonings; mix well.

In another bowl, soak four casings in several changes of cold water to remove the salt they are packed in. Cut the casings with a scissors into 12- to 14-inch lengths if necessary. Keep the remaining casings packed in salt in the refrigerator for future use. If casings are well salted, they can be kept for a month or more.

Slip one end of the casing onto the throat of a sausage funnel. Place the funnel under the kitchen faucet and let cold water run through it. With the water running, slide the casing up onto the funnel, leaving about 3 inches free at the end. Turn off the water and tie a knot in the end of the casing.

Push the sausage meat a little at a time through the funnel with your thumbs. Fill the casing, leaving about 2 inches free at the end to knot; do not pack too tightly. Tie the end and poke holes with a toothpick in the casing to release any air bubbles. Repeat with the remaining sausage meat and casings. Cook or refrigerate for up to 2 days or divide sausage among plastic freezer bags and freeze for future use, up to a year.

GARGANELLI CON ASPARAGI E SALSA DI FORMAGGIO

# Garganelli with Asparagus and Cheese Sauce

SERVES 8 TO 10

*Garganelli, a handmade tubular-shaped pasta with Parmigiano-Reggiano cheese in the dough, gets its classic shape from a comblike device called a* pettine, *which is used to create lines in the dough. Garganelli are usually served with a butter or tomato sauce, but I also like this cream sauce with crispy bits of prosciutto and asparagus. Serve garganelli as an elegant first course for a dinner party. Save time by cooking the asparagus and making the sauce ahead.*

¾ pound asparagus

1¼ teaspoons fine sea salt

1 tablespoon butter

¼ pound prosciutto, diced

1⅓ cups light cream

½ cup freshly grated Parmigiano-Reggiano cheese

1 recipe Garganelli (page 28)

Wash the asparagus and bend the stem with your hands; it will break at just the right point. Discard the woody stems and cut the asparagus in half. Set aside.

Fill a 1-quart saucepan with water and bring to a boil. Add 1 teaspoon of the salt and the asparagus. Cook, uncovered, just until a knife easily pierces the stalk, about 5 minutes. Drain the asparagus in a colander and set aside. (This step can be done ahead and the asparagus refrigerated covered until ready to use.)

Melt the butter in a medium-size sauté pan, taking care not to let it brown. Add the prosciutto and cook slowly over medium heat, stirring occasionally, until the prosciutto is crisp and browned. Remove the prosciutto with a slotted spoon to a dish lined with paper towels. (This step can be done several hours ahead.) Wash out and dry the sauté pan.

Pour the cream into the sauté pan and at low heat stir in the cheese. Stir in the asparagus. Add the remaining ¼ teaspoon salt just before cooking the garganelli.

Cook the garganelli according to the instructions on page 30. Drain the garganelli when *al dente*, reserving 2 tablespoons of the cooking water, and transfer them to a serving platter. Stir the reserved water into the sauce and pour the sauce over the garganelli. Use two serving spoons to mix and evenly distribute the sauce. Scatter the prosciutto over the top and serve immediately.

SEMOLA FRITTA

# Fried Semolina

SERVES 6

*Semola Fritta is another traditional Sardinian dish made with fregola (page 113). Large-size couscous, which is similar to fregola, can be used. The original recipe calls for fresh lard but the substitution of pancetta combined with the taste of spicy salami more than compensates for the omission. The name "semola fritta" is a curious one, since the fregola are not fried at all.*

¼ pound pancetta, diced

2 tablespoons extra virgin olive oil

4¼ cups diced onions (2 large)

4 cups hot water

1½ cups (12 ounces) large *fregola* (*semolina grossa*)

Fine sea salt to taste

½ cup diced sopressata or Genoa salami

Freshly grated Pecorino cheese for sprinkling

In a large pan cook the pancetta with the olive oil over low heat until it begins to crisp, about 4 minutes. Add the onions and cook them slowly until they begin to brown. Pour in the hot water, bring the mixture to a boil, cover the pot, and boil for 15 minutes. Stir in the fregola and mix well with a wooden spoon so they do not stick. Reduce the heat to medium-low and cook until all the liquid is absorbed, about 20 minutes. The semolina should be *al dente*, not mushy; the grains should not be gummy. Stir in the salt and salami. Transfer the mixture to a serving dish, sprinkle on the cheese to taste, and serve.

*Pappardelle con Coniglio, Funghi, e Vino (Pappardelle with Rabbit, Mushrooms, and Wine)*

PAPPARDELLE CON CONIGLIO, FUNGHI, E VINO

# Pappardelle with Rabbit, Mushrooms, and Wine

SERVES 4

*Golden, wide ribbons of noodles known as pappardelle claim Tuscany as home and were originally made to accompany wild duck because woodsmen working in the marshy area of Tuscany known as the Maremma found ducks easy to come by. Boccaccio described pappardelle as lasagne "made two inches thick and cooked in broth and seasoned with meat, especially wild hare." It is also commonly served with wild boar. Pappardelle are easily made from the basic pasta dough recipe on page 9, or can be found on some grocery store shelves. Domestic rabbit is used in this recipe and slowly cooked in the oven in a wine-and-mushroom sauce. Cook the rabbit in the sauce a day ahead to save time if you are making homemade pappardelle.*

¼ cup (½ stick) butter

1 pound mushrooms, wiped clean, stems trimmed, and caps thinly sliced

1 cup dry red wine

½ cup unbleached all-purpose flour

1 teaspoon fine sea salt

Grinding of cracked black pepper

4 pounds cut-up rabbit, washed and dried

2 tablespoons extra virgin olive oil

4 ounces pancetta, diced

1 medium-size red onion, diced

½ pound fennel, bulb only, washed, sliced, and cut into strips

3 cloves garlic, minced

1 tablespoon minced fresh sage leaves

2 tablespoons balsamic vinegar

1 pound homemade (page 21) or store-bought pappardelle

Melt 2 tablespoons of the butter in a large (12 × 3-inch-deep) ovenproof sauté pan or stove-top baking dish large enough to hold all the rabbit pieces. Add the mushrooms and cook over medium-high heat, stirring frequently, until they soften and begin to give off their liquid. Reduce the heat to medium and continue cooking until the liquid evaporates. Increase the heat to high and stir in ½ cup of the wine. Let most of the wine evaporate. Transfer the mushrooms to a bowl and set aside.

Wipe out the sauté pan with a paper towel and return to the stove top.

Mix the flour, salt, and pepper together on a dish. With your hands, dredge each rabbit piece in the flour and shake off the excess. Set aside.

Heat the remaining 2 tablespoons butter and the olive oil in the sauté pan over medium heat and when it is hot, brown the rabbit pieces evenly. Remove the pieces to a dish as they brown.

Add the pancetta to the pan drippings and cook the bits until they begin to brown. Stir in the onion and fennel and cook until the onion softens and the fennel begins to brown. Stir in the garlic and cook 2 to 3

*continued*

minutes more, stirring. Increase the heat to high and stir in the remaining ½ cup wine and the sage leaves. Turn off the heat and stir in the mushrooms with any liquid.

Preheat the oven to 325°F. Tightly cover the pan, place it in the oven, and bake until the rabbit is tender, about 40 minutes. Uncover the pan and stir in the vinegar. Cover and keep the pan warm while the pappardelle cook.

Make and cook homemade pappardelle according to the directions on page 30 or follow the directions for commercially prepared. Drain and place them on a large, deep platter. Spoon the rabbit and mushroom sauce over the pappardelle and serve immediately.

NOTE: *In keeping with Tuscan tradition, I like to use a good Chianti Classico wine in the preparation.*

# Pasta with Shellfish and Fish

SPAGHETTI CON VONGOLE AL CARTOCCIO

# Spaghetti with Clams in Paper

SERVES 4

*Guests will love opening up these rustic-looking parchment bundles of spaghetti with clams. This is a favorite recipe as much for the presentation as well as the taste. Parchment paper keeps the pasta moist, and as soon as the bundles are opened, the escaping aroma brings you right to the seashore. Make the dish as spicy as you would like by controlling the amount of fresh hot pepper added. And be sure to strain the cooking liquid from the clams well to eliminate any sand or grit.*

4 dozen small fresh clams like mahogany or littleneck clams, scrubbed and soaked in several changes of water (discard any with broken shells)

1 cup dry white wine

FOR THE SAUCE

¼ cup olive oil

1 packed cup thinly sliced scallions (about 10)

1 cup thinly sliced fennel, bulb only

2 teaspoons diced seeded jalapeño pepper, or more to taste

2 large cloves garlic, minced

½ cup diced drained Dried Tomatoes in Olive Oil (page 56), or store-bought

¾ teaspoon fine sea salt

¼ teaspoon coarsely ground black pepper

½ cup dry white wine

½ cup chopped fresh Italian parsley leaves

1½ tablespoons freshly squeezed lemon juice

1 pound store-bought spaghetti, linguine, or shells

Cut four sheets of parchment paper into 13 × 22-inch pieces and set aside.

Rinse the clams, place them in a large sauté pan, add the 1 cup of wine, cover the pan, and cook over medium heat just until the clams open. Remove them with a slotted spoon to a bowl. Discard any clams that do not open.

Strain the cooking liquid through damp cheesecloth into a bowl; reserve 1 cup of it, and set it aside. Shuck the clams, leaving eight in their shells. Set aside.

Heat the olive oil in a sauté pan over medium heat. Cook the scallions and fennel, stirring, until the fennel softens; stir in the diced jalapeño and garlic and

cook, stirring occasionally, until the garlic softens but does not brown. Stir in the tomatoes, salt, and pepper and cook for 1 minute. Add the reserved cooking liquid and the ½ cup wine. Stir once or twice, reduce the heat to low, and let the sauce cook, uncovered, for about 5 minutes. Turn off the heat and stir in the parsley, lemon juice, and shucked clams. Cover the pan and keep warm while the spaghetti cooks.

Preheat the oven to 375°F.

Cook the pasta following the directions on page 29. Drain the pasta and add it to the pan with the clams; toss well to distribute the sauce. Divide the mixture among the parchment papers, mounding it in the center of each sheet. Place two of the remaining clams in the shells on top of each sheet. Bring the corners of the parchment paper up and twist them in the center to form a bundle. Tie each with kitchen string.

Place the bundles on a cookie sheet and cook for 10 minutes. Transfer each bundle to four individual shal-low soup bowls and serve immediately, allowing each person to open his or her own bundle.

NOTE: *For a less showy presentation, transfer the pasta and sauce directly to a platter.*

*Spaghetti con Vongole al Cartoccio (Spaghetti with Clams in Paper)*

CAPELLINI D'ANGELI D'EMILIO

# Emilio's Angel Hair Pasta

SERVES 4

*Emilio Maddaloni dishes up his Italian heritage every day in the foods he prepares for his customers. Walking into his store in Portsmouth, New Hampshire, with the stand-up lunch bar is a true leap back in time when things were simple, friendships meant more than schedules, and lunchtime stretched into hours of conversation . . . just remembering. Emilio often makes the meatless dishes of his childhood, which his mother created from nothing and are today the most popular with his clientele. One of his specialties is his mother's angel hair pasta with anchovies, which he further enlivens with jalapeño peppers. Not only is this dish very tasty, it is very quick and, according to Emilio, even better at 3 A.M.*

2 tablespoons extra virgin olive oil

2 cloves garlic, minced

2 tablespoons capers in salt, rinsed and minced

7 or 8 black oil-cured olives, pitted and chopped

4 or 5 anchovy fillets in olive oil, drained, reserving 1 tablespoon of the oil

2 small jalapeño peppers

¼ teaspoon dried red pepper flakes

¼ cup minced fresh Italian parsley leaves

Fine sea salt to taste

½ pound angel hair pasta

Heat the olive oil in a sauté pan, then add the garlic, and cook, stirring, over medium heat until it softens. Stir in the capers, olives, anchovies and reserved oil, jalapeño peppers, red pepper flakes, and half of the parsley, and cook until the anchovies melt into the oil. Add salt as needed. Remove the jalapeño peppers and place in the serving platter. Keep the sauce warm while the pasta cooks.

Cook the angel hair pasta according to directions on page 29. Drain the pasta, reserving ¼ cup of the cooking water. Add the pasta and the reserved water to the sauté pan. Over medium heat quickly stir the pasta and sauce together until well mixed.

Scoop the pasta mixture onto the platter over the jalapeño peppers. Sprinkle the remaining parsley over the top and serve.

FREGOLA CON VONGOLE DI MARIO

# Mario's Fregola with Clams

SERVES 4 TO 6 AS A FIRST COURSE

*Fregola or fregula is a traditional grano duro (hard wheat flour) pasta from Sardinia that resembles couscous. I was introduced to it by my good friends Mario and Giulia Cocco, who make their summer home in Cagliari, one of the four provinces of the island. Mario, who was born in Sardinia, is fiercely proud of his heritage and this dish has been on his family's table for generations. Originally made by hand, and traditionally the work of every bride-to-be, fregola is now commercially made and sold as fregola grossa (large grains) and fregola media (medium grains). Fregola is most frequently served with arselle, the sweet clams of Sardinia. Fregola is not cooked the conventional way in boiling water but added raw to a soffrito (sauté) of olive oil, garlic, and parsley, and cooked slowly with the addition of hot broth and clam juice. According to Mario, this is the best method of cooking and allows the fregola to absorb all the flavors of the ingredients. As with any pasta, fregola should be cooked al dente. It is delicious as a first course, a hearty lunch, and equally as welcome as leftovers. Fregola is available in Italian specialty stores or by mail order (page 160).*

2 pounds fresh clams, scrubbed and soaked in several changes of water (discard any with broken shells)

¼ cup water

¼ cup extra virgin olive oil

2 cloves garlic, minced

¼ cup minced fresh Italian parsley leaves

1 cup fregola (8 ounces)

1 pound fresh or canned (drained) plum tomatoes, peeled

3½ cups hot homemade chicken (page 35) or beef (page 45) or canned low-sodium broth

2 whole Dried Tomatoes in Olive Oil (page 56), cut into pieces

Fine sea salt to taste

Coarsely ground black pepper to taste

Place the clams and water in a medium-size sauté pan. Cover the pan and cook over medium-high heat until the shells open. Remove the clams with a slotted spoon to a dish and set aside until cool enough to handle. Discard any that do not open. Strain the cooking liquid through a cheesecloth-lined strainer into a

bowl, measure out ½ cup, and set aside. Shuck all but five of the clams, chop them coarsely, and set aside.

In a large sauté pan, heat the olive oil over medium heat, then add the garlic and 2 tablespoons of the parsley. Cook, stirring often, until the garlic is deep golden brown (this will give added flavor to the

*continued*

fregola). Add the fregola to the pan and stir to coat the grains well with the olive oil. Add the plum tomatoes and chop them coarsely with a wooden spoon as you stir.

Gradually stir in 3 cups of the broth and the reserved clam juice, allowing the fregola to absorb the liquid as it cooks. The fregola should plump up to double their size and be firm to the bite but cooked through. Add additional broth only if the fregola are still too firm. The fregola should take 20 to 25 minutes to cook.

Two or three minutes before the fregola is ready, add the dried tomatoes and the chopped clams. Stir to blend the ingredients well. Season with salt and pepper. Transfer the fregola to a serving bowl or deep platter. Garnish with the reserved whole clams and sprinkle the remaining 2 tablespoons parsley over the top. Serve immediately.

*Fregola con Vongole di Mario*
*(Mario's Fregola with Clams)*

PIZZA DI PASTA

# *Pasta Pizza*

SERVES 4 TO 6

*How about a pizza di pasta? This dish has all the components without the crust or the cheese! Make this rigatoni and clam dish ahead of time for busy nights; it is easy to put together and can be baked on a pizza pan, cookie sheet, or in a casserole dish. Some advice about clams—cooking them over low heat will prevent them from becoming tough.*

3 tablespoons extra virgin olive oil

2 large cloves garlic, peeled and cut in half lengthwise

Two 10-ounce cans minced clams, drained and liquid reserved

Fine sea salt to taste

¼ teaspoon freshly ground black pepper

¼ cup minced fresh Italian parsley leaves

2 tablespoons minced fresh basil leaves

12 ounces #31 rigatoni, cooked according to the directions on page 29

4 anchovy fillets in oil, drained and cut into bits

1½ cups fresh or canned plum tomatoes (3 or 4), diced

8 oil-cured black olives, pitted and diced

1 teaspoon dried oregano

Preheat the oven to 350°F.

Brush a 14-inch pizza pan with a rim, a 15 × 11½-inch baking sheet, or a 13½ × 9-inch quart ovenproof casserole with 1 teaspoon of the olive oil. Set aside.

In a sauté pan, heat 2 tablespoons of the olive oil and slowly cook the garlic in the oil over medium heat just until it starts to turn golden brown. Remove and discard the garlic. Add the clams and the reserved clam juice. Cook for 2 minutes over medium-low heat. Stir in the salt, pepper, parsley, and basil and cook slowly until the liquid is reduced by half.

Mix the cooked rigatoni with the clam mixture, then spread it evenly over the pizza pan, baking sheet, or casserole. Sprinkle the anchovies over the pasta, then the tomatoes, olives, and oregano. Drizzle the remaining 2 teaspoons olive oil over the top. Bake until heated through, 15 to 20 minutes. Serve at once.

TIP: An olive pitter (*lo snocciolive*) makes quick work out of pitting olives and cherries.

NOTE: *Prepare this dish several hours ahead up to the baking point. Cover with plastic wrap and refrigerate until ready to bake.*

NOTE: *If you prefer a "thicker" pizza, use a 12-inch round pan.*

*Pizza di Pasta
(Pasta Pizza)*

BUCATINI CON BROCCOLI

# Thick Spaghetti with Green Cauliflower

SERVES 4 TO 6

*Broccoflower or green cauliflower is called* broccoli *in Palermo, Sicily, and what we know as broccoli is called* sparaceddi. *It is often combined with a thicker cut of spaghetti called bucatini or perciatelli and flavored with an unusual sauce combination of currants, anchovies, pine nuts, and saffron. Some may be skeptical of the taste, but in this dish, one understands that the Sicilians need look no further than their own island for the ingredients and flavors that have for centuries defined their cuisine.*

¼ cup extra virgin olive oil

1 large onion, diced

3 anchovy fillets in olive oil, drained and minced

1 package (⅟₃₀ ounce or a pinch) powdered saffron dissolved in ¼ cup warm water

½ cup pine nuts

⅓ cup currants or diced raisins

4 to 6 quarts water

2½ tablespoons fine sea salt

1 head green cauliflower (1½ pounds), washed, trimmed, and cut into small florets

1 pound bucatini, perciatelli, or spaghetti

2 tablespoons tomato paste

Heat the olive oil in a deep, large sauté pan, then cook the onion, stirring, over medium heat until it softens. Stir in the anchovies and cook until they dissolve in the pan. Stir in the dissolved saffron. Stir in the pine nuts and currants or raisins and cook for 1 minute. Turn off the heat and set the pan aside.

Bring the 4 to 6 quarts of water to a boil in a pasta pot with an insert. Add 2 tablespoons of the salt and the cauliflower. Cook just until the stems are tender, about 3 minutes. Remove the florets with a slotted spoon and transfer to the pan with the onion mixture.

Cook the bucatini in the same water according to the directions on page 29. Drain the pasta, reserving

½ cup of the cooking water in a small bowl. Transfer the bucatini to the pan with the onion-and-cauliflower mixture and stir to combine the ingredients.

Stir the tomato paste into the reserved water and pour it into the pan with the onions and cauliflower. Add the remaining ½ tablespoon salt, quickly reheat the mixture until hot, and transfer it to a serving dish. Serve immediately.

NOTE: *Instead of purchasing tomato paste in cans, buy it in tube form. This allows you to use the amount you need without having to open a can for just a small amount.*

*Bucatini con Broccoli
(Thick Spaghetti with Green
Cauliflower)*

SALMONE, PISELLI, E PASTA

# Salmon, Peas, and Pasta

SERVES 4 TO 6

*This dish says spring has arrived. The delicate combination of salmon poached in chicken broth and served with a medley of peas, leeks, pepper, and pasta is refreshing with the subtle flavor of orange zest. To save time, poach the salmon up to 2 days in advance.*

3 cups homemade (page 35) or canned low-sodium chicken broth

1 pound salmon fillets, any remaining pin bones pulled out

3 tablespoons extra virgin olive oil

½ pound leeks, white and light green part only, washed well and thinly sliced

1 medium-size red bell pepper, seeded and diced

2 cups fresh or thawed frozen peas

1 teaspoon fine sea salt

1½ tablespoons grated orange zest

1 pound linguine, spaghetti, or other long pasta

Pour the chicken broth into a sauté pan just large enough to hold the salmon fillets in a single layer, or use a salmon poacher if you have one. Bring the broth to a simmer. Poach the salmon, covered, keeping the broth at a simmer. The salmon is cooked when it is uniformly pink-looking and flakes easily with a fork. Do not overcook it; it should remain moist-looking in the center. Remove the salmon with a slotted spoon, place it on a plate, cover, and let cool. Discard all but ¼ cup of the chicken broth.

Heat the olive oil over medium heat in a sauté pan large enough to hold the cooked pasta and salmon mixture. Cook the leeks and red pepper, stirring, until they begin to soften. Add the peas and cook for 1 minute, stirring gently. Remove the pan from the heat and stir in the salt and orange zest. Set aside.

Remove the skin from the underside of the salmon fillet with a knife, then cut it into bite-size pieces and add it to the leek mixture.

Cook the linguine according to the directions on page 29 until *al dente*. Drain the pasta and add it to the leek mixture along with the reserved chicken broth. Reheat the salmon and pasta until hot. Transfer the mixture to a serving platter and serve immediately.

*Salmone, Piselli, e Pasta*
*(Salmon, Peas, and Pasta)*

CALAMARI CON SPAGHETTI E SALSA DI LIMONE E CAPPERI

# Spaghetti with Squid and Lemon Caper Sauce

SERVES 4 TO 6

*This lemon-and-caper sauce with squid is best described as sassy and spicy. To really maximize its flavor, make the sauce several hours before cooking the pasta. Use small-size squid and cook them no longer than 5 minutes or they will become chewy and tough. To save time, prepare the squid the day before making the sauce.*

6 cups water

2 teaspoons fine sea salt

1 pound cleaned small-size squid, cut into ¼-inch-thick rings

2 tablespoons extra virgin olive oil

1 Spanish onion (4 ounces), diced

3 cloves garlic, minced

½ cup minced fresh Italian parsley leaves

1 teaspoon dried red pepper flakes, or more to taste

¼ cup capers in salt, rinsed, drained, and minced

6 tablespoons fresh lemon juice

⅔ cup dry white wine

¼ teaspoon coarse black pepper

1 pound spaghetti, linguine, or fettucine

Bring the water to a boil in a medium-size saucepan. Add 1 teaspoon of salt and squid rings, reduce the heat to medium-high, and cook the rings until tender about 5 minutes. Do not overcook the squid. Drain the rings in a colander and set aside.

In another medium-size saucepan, heat the olive oil, then cook the onion, stirring, until soft but not browned over medium heat. Add the garlic and cook until it softens. Stir in the parsley, red pepper flakes, and capers and cook for 1 minute. Stir in the lemon juice and cook for 2 minutes. Raise the heat to high, stir in the wine, and cook for 1 minute.

Take off the heat and season the sauce with the pepper and the remaining teaspoon of salt. Stir in the squid and mix well. Set aside. This can be done several hours ahead and left to marinate at room temperature.

Cook the spaghetti or linguine according to the directions on page 29.

Meanwhile, reheat the sauce over low heat.

Drain the spaghetti in a colander, reserving 2 tablespoons of the cooking water. Return the spaghetti to the spaghetti pot, stir in the sauce and reserved water, and mix the spaghetti well with the sauce over low heat. Transfer the spaghetti mixture to a platter and serve immediately.

NOTE: *Adjust the amount of red pepper flakes according to taste.*

orzo • pappardelle • penne • quadrucci • ravioli • rotelle • rigatoni • spaghetti • tortellini • trenette • z

# Pasta That Impresses

orzo • pappardelle • penne • quadrucci • ravioli • rotelle • rigatoni • spaghetti • tortellini • trenette • z

## LASAGNE ALLA GRIGLIA CON VERDURE

# Grilled Vegetable Lasagne

SERVES 8

*Purchase a box of no-boil lasagne sheets, grill some summer vegetables, defrost some homemade tomato sauce (page 52), and you will have the components for this unusual preparation for lasagne. It is a good choice for those who are looking for low-fat lasagne, as the only cheese used is Pecorino. You will need a grill to cook the vegetables, but lacking that, roast the vegetables in a preheated 350°F oven on cookie sheets. There are many brands of no-boil lasagne noodles, which eliminates the need to cook the noodles first, but my preference is the Del Verde brand.*

1½ pounds zucchini, washed and sliced into ¼-inch-thick rounds

1 pound eggplant, washed and cut into ¼-inch-thick rounds

1 large onion, unpeeled and cut into quarters

Olive oil or olive oil spray

3 cups prepared tomato sauce

8 no-boil lasagne sheets (6½ × 7 inches)

Fine sea salt to taste

Freshly ground black pepper to taste

½ cup freshly grated Pecorino cheese

Preheat the grill.

Spray or brush the vegetables on both sides lightly with olive oil. Grill the vegetables in batches if necessary until soft and grill marks appear. Turn once during the cooking time. Transfer the vegetables to a bowl. Remove the skin from the onion and cut it into thin slices. Set the vegetables aside.

Preheat the oven to 350°F.

Spread ⅓ cup of the tomato sauce in a 13½ × 9-inch Pyrex or other similar baking dish. Place two lasagne sheets side by side in the pan. Make a single layer of eggplant over the sheets. Scatter a third of the sliced onion over the eggplant. Salt and pepper the layer and spread ½ cup of tomato sauce over it. Sprinkle 2 tablespoons of the cheese evenly over the top. Cover the eggplant layer with two more lasagne sheets. Make a single layer of zucchini over the sheets. Scatter on half of the remaining onion, season with salt and pepper, and spread another ½ cup of tomato sauce over. Place two more sheets of lasagne noodles over the tomato sauce and make the final layer of vegetables with the remaining zucchini and eggplant. Scatter on the rest of the onion, season with salt and pepper, sprinkle with 2 tablespoons of the cheese, and ½ cup of the tomato sauce. Cover with the final two sheets of lasagne noodles, spread the remaining sauce over the top, and sprinkle the remaining cheese over the sauce. Tightly cover the dish with a sheet of aluminum foil. Bake until the noodles are soft, 35 to 40 minutes.

Let the lasagne sit for 10 minutes before cutting into pieces. Serve immediately.

NOTE: *Cooked lasagne should always be stored in the refrigerator with a sheet of wax paper between the lasagne and aluminum foil to keep the acid in the tomatoes from reacting with the foil.*

*Lasagne alla Griglia con Verdure (Grilled Vegetable Lasagne)*

## CANNELLONI ALL'ERBE DI PREZZEMOLO E BASILICO
# Parsley and Basil Cannelloni

SERVES 10

*Cylinders of homemade pasta embedded with fresh whole leaves of parsley and basil give a beautiful artistic look to these light-tasting cheese and vegetable stuffed cannelloni, and although cannelloni rightfully belong in the category of traditional pasta, they achieve a stylish presentation in this almost wrapping-paper look with pressed herbs in the dough. This is the perfect* primo piatto *(first course) when an elegant dinner is called for. The filling can be prepared two days ahead and the whole dish can be assembled a day in advance or frozen for future use.*

### FOR THE FILLING
2 pounds ricotta cheese, well drained

1 small zucchini, grated to make 1 cup

1 small carrot, grated to make ½ cup

½ cup freshly grated Parmigiano-Reggiano cheese

2 tablespoons grated lemon zest (2 large lemons)

2 teaspoons fine sea salt

¼ teaspoons freshly grated nutmeg

### FOR THE PASTA
1 recipe Handmade Pasta dough (page 9)

1 large egg white, slightly beaten

Several sprigs fresh Italian parsley, damp-wiped and stemmed

Several sprigs fresh small basil leaves, damp-wiped and stemmed

4 quarts water

1 tablespoon salt

### FOR THE SAUCE
1 cup (2 sticks) unsalted butter, melted

1 cup freshly grated Parmigiano-Reggiano cheese

Combine all the filling ingredients in a large bowl, cover, and refrigerate until ready to use.

Divide the pasta dough into quarters; work with one quarter at a time and keep the rest covered under a bowl on a lightly floured surface. Knead the dough for a few minutes on a lightly floured work surface. Flatten the dough with a rolling pin, then thin it in a hand-crank pasta machine following the directions on page 11 for rolling the dough. Trim the thinned dough to 30 inches long and cut it in half. Save any scraps for re-rolling.

Lightly brush one half of the sheet with the beaten egg white. Arrange a few leaves of parsley and basil along the length of the sheet, pressing them lightly

*Cannelloni all'Erbe di Prezzemolo e Basilico*
*(Parsley and Basil Cannelloni)*

into the dough. This will help the herbs to adhere and not fall out of the dough when put through the pasta machine. Top with the second sheet of dough. Thin the sheet again between the rollers to 25 inches. Cut five 5-inch squares from the dough and arrange them on a kitchen-towel-lined cookie sheet.

Continue with the rest of the dough. As the strips are cut, layer them over more kitchen towels; do not put them directly on top of the first layer or they will stick together.

Fill a baking dish with cold water and add a few ice cubes. Set aside.

Bring the 4 quarts water to a boil in a pasta pot without the insert. Add the salt, then cook half a dozen strips at a time about 1 minute; they will quickly rise to the surface. Use a pasta scoop to lift the strips from the pot and transfer them to the dish with the ice water. As soon as they are cool enough to handle, transfer the strips to clean kitchen towels and, with another towel, blot them dry.

Lightly butter two 13½ × 9-inch baking dishes. Set aside.

Spread about ¼ cup of the filling along the length of each strip; roll them up into cylinders and place them seam side down in the baking dish.

At this point the cannelloni can be wrapped and refrigerated and cooked the following day or they can be sealed in aluminium foil and frozen for up to 3 months. Frozen cannelloni do not need to be defrosted, but the baking time will be increased by 10 to 12 minutes.

To bake immediately, melt the butter and pour it evenly over the tops of the cannelloni. Sprinkle the cheese evenly over the top. Cover the baking dishes with aluminum foil and bake the cannelloni for about 15 minutes. Remove the dishes from the oven and turn on the broiler. Remove the aluminum foil and broil the cannelloni just until the cheese begins to brown. Remove and serve immediately, allowing two cannelloni per person as a first course. Pass additional cheese for sprinkling on top.

TIP: Use the small holes on a four-sided cheese grater to grate the vegetables or the grating disk in a food processor.

TIP: Be sure the stems are completely detached from the parsley and basil or they will cause the dough to rip when it is thinned.

NOTE: *Nonfat ricotta cheese also works well, but increase the amount of salt by ½ teaspoon.*

# Making Parsley and Basil Cannelloni

*Brushing the sheet of dough with egg white.*

*Placing the fresh herb leaves on the sheet of dough.*

*Placing the second sheet over the herbs.*

*Thinning the sandwiched dough in the pasta machine.*

*Cutting the thinned-out dough into 5-inch squares.*

*Spreading the filling over the cooked pasta squares.*

*Rolling up the cannelloni and placing them in the baking dish.*

INVOLTINI DI MELANZANE E CAPELLINI

# Eggplant and Angel Hair Bundles

SERVES 6

*Here is a good example of choosing the right pasta as a filling. Strips of eggplant become the cylindrical container for neatly packaged angel hair pasta. Involtini makes a great presentation on a buffet table, and can be prepared a day in advance.*

3½ tablespoons extra virgin olive oil

One 9-inch-long eggplant, washed and cut lengthwise into ¼-inch-thick slices

1 medium-size onion, diced

¼ pound prosciutto, diced

8 ounces (4 nests) angel hair pasta

¼ pound caciocavallo cheese, diced (see Note)

½ cup diced Dried Tomatoes in Olive Oil (page 56)

⅓ cup diced pitted oil-cured black olives

Fine sea salt to taste

Freshly ground black pepper to taste

Preheat the oven to 350°F.

Lightly brush a 9 × 12-inch baking dish with olive oil and set aside.

Brush two baking sheets with 1 tablespoon of the olive oil. Lay the eggplant slices in single layers on the sheets. Bake until soft enough to roll up, 10 to 12 minutes. Do not let the slices brown or they will be too dry to roll.

Meanwhile, in a large sauté pan over medium heat, heat the remaining 2 tablespoons olive oil, then add the onion and prosciutto and cook, stirring, until the onion is soft and the prosciutto begins to brown. Transfer the mixture to a large bowl.

Cook the angel hair according to the directions on page 29. Drain and add it to the onion mixture, tossing well. Mix in the cheese, tomatoes, and olives and season with salt and pepper.

Divide the angel hair mixture evenly among the eggplant slices, spreading the mixture the length of the slices. Roll each slice up like a jelly roll and place seam side down the prepared 9 × 12-inch baking dish. Cover the dish tightly with aluminum foil and bake until the bundles are hot, 20 to 25 minutes. Serve immediately.

NOTE: *Caciocavallo is a cow's milk cheese with a stringy consistency. If unavailable, substitute provolone—either sharp or mild.*

## PANZEROTTI BILACUS
# Stuffed Pasta Bilacus Style

MAKES ABOUT 3½ DOZEN

*If you are lucky enough to travel sometime to Bellagio on Lago di Como (Lake Como), head for Ristorante Bilacus on Via Serbelloni. As soon as you cross the threshold, you will know that you are in a restaurant that is serious about the food it serves because a sign over the doorway proudly proclaims this establishment as a "club, del Buongustaio," a club of good taste. My favorite first course is panzerotti, neat cylinders of almost translucent pasta filled with exquisite creamy ricotta and Taleggio cheese and flecked with bits of* prosciutto di Parma.

*To save time, make the filling a day ahead and refrigerate. The whole dish can be assembled ahead of time and baked later or the next day. For longer storage, freeze the panzerotti well wrapped with aluminum foil. These are very rich and three per person is adequate as a first course or a buffet item.*

### FOR THE FILLING
5½ (44 ounces) cups whole-milk or skim-milk ricotta cheese

¾ cup diced Taleggio cheese (see Note), rind removed

½ pound *prosciutto di Parma* or ham, diced

### FOR THE PASTA AND TO FINISH
1 recipe Handmade Pasta dough (page 9)

2 tablespoons butter

4 to 6 quarts water

1 tablespoon salt

### FOR THE SAUCE
1 cup (2 sticks) unsalted butter, melted

1 cup freshly grated Parmigiano-Reggiano cheese

Combine all the filling ingredients in a large bowl, cover, and refrigerate until needed.

Divide the pasta dough into four pieces. Work with one piece at a time, keeping the remainder on a lightly floured surface covered under a bowl. Flatten each piece slightly with a rolling pin to about 6 inches wide (which will fit the width of a standard pasta machine), then thin the pieces in a pasta machine to the thickness of typing paper following the directions on page 11. Trim each piece to 30 inches. Reserve the scraps to re-roll. With a pastry wheel, divide the sheet lengthwise into two 3-inch-wide strips and cut each strip into five 6-inch-long pieces. As you make the strips, place them in a single layer on clean kitchen towels.

Lightly grease three 14½ × 9-inch Pyrex baking pans with the 2 tablespoons of butter and set aside.

*continued*

Fill a large shallow pan with ice water and set aside.

Bring the 4 to 6 quarts water to a boil. Add the salt, then cook eight strips at a time for just 2 minutes. Use a skimmer spoon to lift the strips from the water and place them in the pan of ice water. This will allow them to cool down and make them easier to handle. Lift the strips from the ice water and place them on a kitchen towel in a single layer. Repeat with the remaining pasta strips.

Spread 2 generous tablespoons of the filling over each pasta strip. Roll each strip up into a cylinder and place seam side down in the prepared baking dishes. At this point the dishes can be covered tightly with plastic wrap, refrigerated for up to 2 days, and baked when needed.

When ready to bake, preheat the oven to 350°F. Remove the plastic wrap from the baking dish, pour one third of the melted butter over the panzerotti in each pan, divide and sprinkle cheese over the top of each pan, cover each pan tightly with aluminum foil, and bake until heated through, 20 to 25 minutes. Serve immediately.

NOTE: *Taleggio cheese comes from Lombardia and is a soft, high-fat cow's milk cheese with a reddish brown rind. The cheese is delicious on its own or with ripe pears but works wonderfully as a melted cheese in many main dishes. Substitute Italian Fontina in this recipe if Taleggio is unavailable.*

NOTE: *Sometimes I add bits of chopped fresh tomatoes when in season as a garnish.*

*lletti • bucatini • capellini • ditalini • farfalle • fettucine • fregola • fusilli • lasagne • linguine • maltag*

# The Count and I

I really had no intention of taking a long bus trip with a group of Italian food experts that day, but the allure of having a seafood feast at the famed Hotel L'Approdo in Santa Maria de Leuca in Puglia was too much to resist. So on a gorgeous sunny day the trip from Lecce began on route ss275.

The ride was mesmerizing as groves and groves of olive trees lined the roadway, each one an individual statement on just how important olive oil is to this region. As we approached the hotel, a dazzling blue sea rose up to greet us. Truly this was paradise, and worth a bus trip to get to.

As promised, lunch was an extravaganza of local fish dishes and we dined on a wide terrace overlook-

ing a brilliant blue sea that contrasted beautifully against whitewashed buildings. Everything from spiny lobster to *orata,* a flat fish with a delicate flavor cooked simply with a few herbs, lemon juice, and, of course, olive oil, was delicious. *Dentice* (sea bream), considered a prize fish, was my favorite and the *frutta di mare* with delicate octopus and squid had us all sopping up the juices from our plates

*lletti • bucatini • capellini • ditalini • farfalle • fettucine • fregola • fusilli • lasagne • linguine • malta*

with hunks of earthy Pugliese bread.

After that wonderful interlude, which left us all beyond satiated, we boarded the bus for the long trip back to Lecce and a night of quiet rest. Once off the bus I made a quick departure from the group toward my room when a friend asked if I would say hello to a group of wine makers from a nearby winery in Leverano. The group included the owner of the vineyards, Count Zecca. The count wanted us to see his vineyards because he was interested in introducing his wines, Zecci wines, into the United States. How could I refuse? And laid to rest any plans I had for a hot shower and an evening of Italian television.

The count was a tall, elegant-looking man with thick silver hair, piercing sea-blue eyes, and a ruddy face reminiscent of Clint Eastwood. After handshakes and a round of *"Piacere"* (pleasure to meet you), a small group of us drove to the winery, me being the count's guest in the front seat of his Mercedes. Now instead of just relaxing after a long day of bus travel, I found myself the translator for the group since no one spoke Italian and mine was average at best. We talked of the count's family involvement in the wine business, his ancestors, the weather, and, of course, the food of Puglia.

Finally arriving at the winery, we were given a tour where we learned that the count makes red, white, frizzante, and a rosé wine using *negro amaro* and *malvasia nero* grapes. The winery turned out about one million liter bottles a year.

After the tour I assumed we would return to the hotel. I looked as if I had been camping in the woods for a week and longed for a shower. Instead, the count surprised us by his kind invitation to dinner. To dinner! We had just hours before consumed the consummate lunch but it was obvious that we could not be rude, so we drove to his sixteenth-century *palazzo*. Once the door was opened I knew that we had entered a world few would ever have the privilege of experiencing. Venetian glass chandeliers in the entryway had us gasping with delight. The walls were decorated with gilt and held precious portraits of the count's ancestors as well as exquisite European art. The floors were covered in vibrant-colored handmade tiles from Campania.

We were ushered into the parlor where the count introduced us to his brother and his wife and a woman simply referred to as the count's companion. We tasted the count's wines and nibbled on aged Parmigiano-Reggiano cheese, *tarallini*, which were bite-size hard biscuits resembling bagels, local *salame*, and onion *taralli* in the shape of cubes.

Dinner was served in the elegant dining room lit by another Venetian glass chandelier. There were thirteen of us in all, but I had the seat of honor next to the count and knew that while the others enjoyed their meal, I would be answering questions between mouthfuls of food. I assumed we would start with a typical pasta of the region, orecchiette (little ears), served with some type of bitter green with the intensely flavored olive oil that Puglia is known for. So I was surprised when Therea, the count's longtime cook, made her entrance dressed in a maid's black uniform with white starched apron, white gloves, and cap, and began serving ravioli from a silver bowl; they were filled with fresh ricotta cheese and spinach and topped with a butter-and-sage sauce and they were superb. The dough was so thin and light that I found myself regretting that I had said *"un po"* (just a little), for I could have eaten more of them. After that came *orata*, baked whole fish cooked with olive oil and lemon that I had also enjoyed just hours ago at lunch. This was accompanied by whole baby potatoes served with a velvety homemade mayonnaise; the potatoes were so creamy that they nearly melted in your mouth. An *insalata mista* followed and was served with the count's own olive oil and wine vinegar. Bread called *pane casalingo,* a large round coarse-grained type that is made to last a week, was also served.

During the course of dinner, the count asked me about my previous travels in Italy and where my ancestors came from. I found myself constructing every Italian word carefully before I replied.

I thought nothing could top those elegant ravioli, but then came the *bocconcini* (little fresh mozzarella balls), served with a drizzle of double cream and a chiffonnade of fresh basil. The count preferred to call them mozzarella *di Campania.*

Dessert was elegant in its simplicity: tiny wild strawberries and homemade vanilla gelato with whipped cream lying in soft layers in a large antique glass bowl. I could hardly believe that I had dined at a count's table and enjoyed another huge meal and I said a silent prayer in gratitude for the experience.

We adjourned to the parlor where the count served after-dinner liqueurs and more wine. As we talked about our impressions of Puglia and its food, Jeff, one of the American dinner guests who taught cooking in California and was a tenor as well, asked me if I would beg the count's indulgence and permit him to sing a song in appreciation for the count's hospitality. This done, I assumed that he was going to sing some classic operatic piece familiar to the count. I sat back and relaxed but only for a moment as he belted out a spirited rendition of "Ol' Man River." I winced, hard, then glanced at the count, who, in a gracious way, had a very puzzled look on his face. For me it was the longest rendition of "Ol' Man River" that I had heard in a long time. The count nodded his appreciation as more wine was poured and conversation resumed in earnest. Then he asked me to join him in the hallway; he wanted to give me a tour of the *palazzo.* I was curious as to why the others were not coming too. He took my arm and I felt like Cinderella at the ball.

He was especially interested in showing me the *cantina,* and the various rooms of the *palazzo.* We walked arm-in-arm out onto the portico where the count asked me about my last name, Esposito, a Spanish as well as Italian name, which I explained to him was my married name. We talked of the Spanish-Bourbon influence in Italy.

Still arm-in-arm we examined some of the count's antique book collection in the library and more portraits of his ancestors. We had been gone from the group for what seemed like hours and as we made our way back to the parlor I had a distinct feeling that all eyes were upon me and all minds were asking the same silent questions.

Finally, it was time to say good-bye and I thought that would be the last time that I would see the count when he surprised us by offering to drive us back to our hotel.

Once again I took my designated place in the front seat and made small talk as we drove the few miles back. I promised to keep in touch with the count as I got out of the car and gestured to shake his hand but instead he planted a very nice kiss upon it. So chivalrous, I thought. I thanked him again for his warm hospitality, the unforgettable evening, and, of course, delicious food. I turned and walked into the hotel. Before going to bed, I scribbled the events of the whirlwind day in my journal and heavily underlined the words: "The Count is a dream—tall, piercing blue eyes and silver-gray hair. Make the Count's ravioli."

RAVIOLI SQUISITI DEL CONTE ZECCA

# Count Zecca's Exquisite Ravioli

MAKES AT LEAST 10 DOZEN (SERVES 15 TO 20 AS A FIRST COURSE)

*These are the exquisite ricotta-cheese-and-spinach-filled ravioli with butter-and-sage sauce served as a first course at Count Alichiedi Zecca's dinner party. Use the best whole-milk ricotta cheese available; to give the filling the creamy taste of the original, heavy cream has been added. Plan on six to eight ravioli per person and cook only as much as you need. The ravioli can be made ahead and frozen uncooked for future use.*

**FOR THE FILLING** *(makes 3 cups)*

1 pound fresh spinach, stemmed, washed well, and torn into pieces, or one 10-ounce package frozen spinach, thawed, cooked according to the package directions, and squeezed dry

2 cups ricotta cheese

1 large egg

6 tablespoons freshly grated Parmigiano-Reggiano cheese

3 tablespoons heavy cream

¼ teaspoon fine sea salt

**FOR THE PASTA**

1 recipe Handmade Pasta dough (page 9)

**FOR THE SAUCE**
*(enough to sauce 5 dozen)*

½ cup (1 stick) unsalted butter, melted

6 large fresh sage leaves, minced

If using fresh spinach, place the leaves in a large skillet with just the water clinging to their leaves. Cover and cook over medium heat just until the leaves are wilted, about 2 minutes. Drain the spinach into a colander and, when cool enough to handle, squeeze as much water out as possible. Mince the spinach (fresh or the cooked frozen spinach) and place it in a bowl. Stir in the remaining filling ingredients and blend well. Cover and refrigerate the filling while you make the dough.

Divide the dough into four pieces; work with one piece at a time and keep the rest covered under a bowl on a lightly floured surface.

To make ravioli using the pasta machine and a ravioli form, thin the dough to the next to last setting on the machine (page 11). Trim the dough to fit over the teeth of a 12-inch-long ravioli form, leaving about a ½-inch overhang (see the technique on page 136). After making a slight impression in the dough with the top of the ravioli form, place a scant teaspoon of filling in each impression. Cover with a second sheet of dough and, with a rolling pin, roll over the top of the form, pressing down firmly to cut the ravioli. Turn the form over and gently push the ravioli out with your fingers. Place them on kitchen-towel-lined baking sheets and repeat with the remaining dough and filling.

To make ravioli by hand, roll each piece of dough into a 12 × 10-inch rectangle (page 137). With a ruler and a table knife, carefully measure and score five rows

# Making ravioli with a ravioli form

Laying a thinned-out sheet of dough over the form.

Placing the top of the form on the sheet of dough and making an impression.

The impressions.

Filling the impressions.

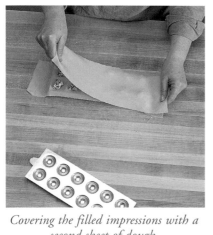

Covering the filled impressions with a second sheet of dough.

Rolling over the form to cut and separate the ravioli.

Pushing the ravioli out of the form.

of six 2-inch squares. Be sure not to cut through the dough. Place a scant teaspoon of the filling in the center of each square. Roll out a second piece of dough of the same dimensions and carefully place over the top of the filling. Gently press down between the rows with your hands and seal the edges. Use a pastry wheel to cut between the rows lengthwise as well as widthwise.

To cook, heat the butter with the sage leaves for the sauce and keep warm.

Follow the directions for cooking fresh filled pasta on page 30. Drain the ravioli carefully using a pasta scoop. Place them in a shallow platter. Pour the butter-and-sage sauce over them and toss carefully to coat the ravioli. Serve immediately.

To freeze the uncooked ravioli, place them on flour-dusted baking sheets in single rows. Loosely cover the sheets with aluminum foil and place them in the freezer until the ravioli are hard. Transfer the ravioli to plastic bags, seal, and freeze.

*Making ravioli without a form*

*Spacing the filling out on a thinned-out sheet of dough.*

*Covering the filling with a second sheet of dough.*

*Pressing down between the rows to seal the edges.*

*Using a pastry wheel to cut between the rows of ravioli.*

TORTELLI DI PATATE E RICOTTA

# Half-Moon Pasta with Potatoes and Ricotta Cheese

MAKES ABOUT 16 DOZEN

*Tortelli (anolini) are filled half-moon-shaped pasta from the region of Emilia-Romagna. Some of the best I have ever eaten were sampled in Mamiano, in the Fondazione Magnani Rocca, after visiting a fabulous art collection belonging to the late Luigi Magnani and supported by the Consorzio del Formaggio Parmigiano-Reggiano. There were several kinds of tortelli on the menu, some filled with Swiss chard, others with pumpkin, and these potato-and-ricotta-cheese ones flavored with the famed Parmigiano-Reggiano cheese of the region and just a hint of nutmeg. Tortelli are traditionally served with butter and more cheese. They are time consuming to make, but the filling can be prepared a day ahead, the dough can be made in a food processor, and the tortelli can be frozen for several months. Tortelli are eaten as a first course, usually eight to ten per serving.*

### FOR THE TORTELLI
*(makes about 3⅓ cups filling, enough for 16 dozen)*

1 pound potatoes, peeled and cut into chunks

½ pound ricotta cheese, well drained

1 large egg

1 teaspoon fine sea salt

½ teaspoon freshly grated nutmeg

1 recipe Handmade Pasta dough (page 9)

4 quarts water per each 4 dozen tortelli

1 tablespoon salt

### FOR THE SAUCE
*(enough for 4 dozen tortelli)*

½ cup (1 stick) unsalted butter, melted

¼ cup plus 2 tablespoons freshly grated Parmigiano-Reggiano cheese

Cover the potatoes with cold water in a medium-size saucepan, bring to a boil, and boil until a knife slides easily into them. Drain the potatoes, transfer them to a large bowl, and mash them with a hand masher until smooth. Stir in the ricotta cheese, egg, salt, and nutmeg. Set the mixture aside.

Divide the dough into four pieces and work with one piece at a time, keeping the remaining pieces under a bowl.

If making the tortelli by hand roll each piece with a rolling pin into a 14-inch circle. Using a 2-inch fluted round cutter, cut circles from the dough as close together as possible. Gather up the scraps and re-roll to make more circles. Place ¼ teaspoon of the potato filling in the center of each circle. Fold the circle in half to make a half-moon or crescent shape and pinch the edges together to form a tight seal so the filling will not ooze out. If the dough seems dry, brush the edges with a little water before sealing them. Place the tortelli on kitchen-towel-lined cookie sheets in single layers. Continue making tortelli with the remaining dough and filling.

If using a pasta machine, roll each piece of dough with a rolling pin to flatten it slightly, then thin the dough through the rollers of the pasta machine to the thinnest setting according to the directions on page 11. Cut out circles and fill as above. Gather up and re-roll the scraps to make more tortelli.

Fill a pasta pot with an insert with the water. When the water boils, add the salt and tortelli and cook for 2 to 3 minutes.

Meanwhile, melt the butter in a small saucepan, add the cheese, pour the sauce into a serving bowl or platter, and keep warm.

Use a pasta scoop to drain the tortelli. Transfer them to the warm serving dish and toss gently with the sauce. Serve immediately

TIP: Keep several wet paper towels handy to wipe your hands as you are filling the tortelli so they will be clean to pinch the edges closed.

NOTE: *To freeze for future use, cover the uncooked tortelli with a sheet of plastic wrap and place in the freezer on the towel-lined cookie sheet until hard. Transfer the tortelli to heavy-duty plastic bags and freeze. Do not defrost the tortelli before cooking them. Bring the water to a rolling boil before cooking them. They will take about 2 minutes longer to cook than freshly made.*

letti • bucatini • capellini • ditalini • farfalle • fettucine • fregola • fusilli • lasagne • linguine • malta

## Tortelli, Tortellini, and Tortelloni

In the region of Emilia-Romagna in the city of Reggio Emilia stands a delightful pasta shop on Via Antonio Franzoni affectionately called Casalinga (meaning homemade), where proud women gifted in the art of patience and attention to detail stand for hours in starched, snowy white aprons and caps making tortelli, tortellini, and tortelloni with hands that appear to move at lightning speed. Rules and fussiness define the finished product and these three hallmark fresh filled pastas, along with lasagne, reach their zenith in Emilia-Romagna. The appetite that people there have for them is so great that it has been said that it is far better for them to have to live each day without sunshine than to live each day without their beloved tortellini, tortelli, and tortelloni. Numerous shops throughout the city cater to the daily demand of their customers with huge display windows filled to the brim with the sunny yellow egg-rich stuffed dough that by day's end will be all but depleted.

Tortelli, which are similar to ravioli, can vary in shape and filling from one locale to another, and that is also part of their charm, for it gives added credence to the fact that there is no standard formula for what is called Italian cuisine. For example, the great native Romagnan gastronome and food writer Pellegrino Artusi described tortelli as made in the shape of a half moon or in the shape of little hats called cappelletti stuffed with meat fillings. In Reggio Emilia, tortelli are square and filled with squash and crushed amaretti cookies, or ricotta cheese and spinach, or potato and ricotta cheese. In the nearby city of Cremona they are triangular and filled with squash and crushed *mostaccino,* a locally made spicy cookie.

Tortellini are small pasta rings stuffed with finely ground meats such as capon, pork, chicken, turkey, mortadella, and prosciutto and are traditionally served in capon broth, but they are also offered under blankets of cream sauce and as the filling for *pasticcio,* in which a rich pastry dough becomes the container for tortellini and the whole pie is baked.

Tortelloni are large-size tortelli that are most frequently filled with creamy ricotta cheese, Parmigiano-Reggiano cheese, parsley, and nutmeg. Tortelli and tortelloni are served with a butter-and-cheese sauce, although occasionally sage is added, and some cooks like to use a light tomato sauce.

Today the tradition of making these filled pastas at home is nearly a thing of the past, since time and patience are two other necessary ingredients for creating them. No Emilia-Romagna Christmas dinner would be complete without tortellini as a *primo piatto* (first course). It has not been determined how far back the association of tortellini with the holidays began, but according to Waverly Root's work *The Food of Italy,* it was a custom as far back as the thirteenth century to give tortellini as a gift to members of the clergy.

The success of making tortelli, tortellini, and tortelloni lies in the thickness of the dough; it must not be rolled so thin that the filling will burst through when cooked, nor rolled so thick that the dough is chewy and dense and all but masks the flavor of the filling, which must be moist and flavorful with just the right ratio of filling to dough. If you can see the outline of your hand when held behind a sheet of rolled-out pasta, the dough is thin enough. The dough must also not be too dry, otherwise it will be difficult to seal the edges.

Since making these pastas is very time consuming, try staging the process by making the filling 2 days before making the pasta. Then make, fill, and shape the pasta several hours before cooking and place the tortelli, tortellini, or tortelloni on kitchen towels in single layers.

These can also be frozen and kept for up to 4 months if well sealed. After forming the pasta and placing them in single layers, cover the trays loosely with aluminum foil and place them in the freezer until the pasta hardens, then place the pieces in plastic bags and freeze. Take out as many as you wish to cook, putting the frozen pasta directly into boiling water but cooking only a few dozen at a time so as not to bring the temperature of the water down too much. Use a slotted spoon or pasta scoop to drain the pasta from the water and keep them warm while cooking the rest. Dress with the appropriate sauce and serve immediately.

## TIMBALLO DI MELANZANE E BUCATINI

# A Drum of Eggplant and Bucatini

SERVES 10 TO 12

*Making a* timballo, *or* timpano, *is an event. It becomes the moment in which ordinary ingredients like macaroni, cheese, and vegetables are transformed into an extraordinary, impressive drum of baked pasta that, when unmolded, receives a standing ovation. The region of Campania claims the* timballo *as its own and the recipe that follows comes from Sorrento. It calls for bucatini, a thicker cut of hollow spaghetti, which neatly nestles and holds the ingredients together. It is customary in Campania to use buffalo milk mozzarella, a cheese with a delicate texture and superb taste, but it is very perishable and not readily available. Fresh cow's milk mozzarella can be used instead.*

*Assembling the* timballo *is easy when done in stages. Make the sauce several days ahead; cube the cheese and cook the marble-size meatballs 2 days ahead. Patience is the key to the unmolding; you will get much neater wedges by allowing the* timballo *to cool for about 20 minutes—and the joy of tasting that first forkful will be worthy of the best drumroll.*

3 large eggplants (each at least 11 inches long)

Salt

½ cup Toasted Bread Crumbs (page 89)

### FOR THE SAUCE

2 tablespoons extra virgin olive oil

¼ cup finely chopped onions

1 large carrot, finely chopped

1 rib celery, finely chopped

3 cloves garlic, minced

5 cups chopped fresh or canned (drained) plum tomatoes (about 10 medium size)

¼ cup dry red wine

1 bay leaf

1½ teaspoons fine sea salt

Freshly ground black pepper to taste

### FOR THE FILLING

2 cups bucatini broken into thirds

1 pound ground veal

1 large egg, beaten

2 tablespoons dry white wine

2 tablespoons freshly grated Pecorino cheese

½ cup Toasted Bread Crumbs

1 teaspoon fine sea salt

2 tablespoons butter

1½ cups cubed fresh mozzarella (*fior di latte*) cheese

¼ cup chopped fresh Italian parsley leaves

½ cup peanut oil for frying

¼ cup freshly grated Pecorino cheese

*continued*

Cut off the stems of the eggplants and discard. Slice the eggplant lengthwise into ¼-inch-thick slices. Salt and layer the eggplant slices in a colander set over a bowl. Place a large bowl of water on top of the slices to act as a weight. Let the eggplant "sweat" for at least 1 hour to remove the excess water.

Butter a 9 × 3½-inch-deep round mold or cake pan and coat the inside evenly with the ½ cup bread crumbs. Shake out the excess crumbs and refrigerate the mold until ready to fill.

To make the sauce: In a large saucepan, heat the olive oil and cook, stirring, the onions, carrot, and celery until they soften. Add the garlic and cook, stirring, until the garlic softens. Stir in the tomatoes, red wine, and bay leaf. Cover the pan and simmer the sauce for 30 minutes. Season with salt and pepper and set aside. Remove the bay leaf before using.

Cook the bucatini according to the directions on page 29. Drain and transfer to a large bowl. Set aside.

In a medium-size bowl, combine the veal, egg, white wine, the 2 tablespoons grated Pecorino, bread crumbs, and salt. Mix gently to just combine the ingredients. Form marble-size meatballs with your hands.

Heat the butter in a large sauté pan and fry the meatballs until browned on all sides. Transfer the meatballs to the bowl with the bucatini. Add the mozzarella, parsley, and 2 cups of the tomato sauce. Stir to combine the ingredients well and set aside.

Rinse and dry the eggplant slices. Heat the peanut oil in a large sauté pan over medium-high heat. Fry the eggplant slices a few at a time until they soften, about 2 minutes on each side. Drain the slices on brown paper. Use additional oil if the pan seems dry.

Preheat the oven to 325°F.

Line the prepared mold with the eggplant slices, draping them lengthwise over the bottom and overlapping them up the sides of the mold. There should be about a 3-inch overhang over the top edges of the mold. Make sure there are no open spots and that the mold is completely lined with the slices.

Spoon the bucatini mixture evenly in the mold, packing it down with a wooden spoon all the way around. Fold the overhanging slices of eggplant in over the top of the mold; the mixture should be completely encased by the eggplant.

Spread ½ cup of the remaining tomato sauce over the top of the mold and sprinkle with the ¼ cup Pecorino. Bake the *timballo*, uncovered, for 45 minutes. It is done when the *timballo* shrinks a bit along the sides and a knife will easily move along the sides. Remove the mold from the oven and loosely cover the top with a sheet of aluminum foil. Let the mold stand for 20 minutes.

Heat the remaining tomato sauce. Remove the foil from the *timballo* and run a butter knife around the inside edges to loosen it. Place a serving dish larger than the mold over the top and carefully invert it onto the dish. Cut the *timballo* into wedges and serve with additional sauce on the side.

TIP: Use fresh mozzarella cheese, but if it is not available, substitute pasteurized.

NOTE: *Instead of frying the meatballs, bake them on a lightly greased cookie sheet at 350°F until nicely browned, about 20 minutes.*

NOTE: *For a nice presentation, spread additional sauce over the top of the unmolded* timballo *and garnish with curls of Pecorino cheese.*

*Timballo di Melanzane e Bucatini (A Drum of Eggplant and Bucatini) (page 141)*

*Timballo di Farfalla e Fava (Butterfly Pasta and Fava Bean Mold)*

## TIMBALLO DI FARFALLA E FAVA
# Butterfy Pasta and Fava Bean Mold

SERVES 8

*A* timballo *is a combination of ingredients, usually with some type of pasta, baked in a mold or springform pan and then unmolded. Some* timballi *are chock-full of ingredients while others rely on just a few. Nevertheless, they are impressive-looking and can even be made using ovenproof glass bowls. Farfalle (butterflies) and fava beans flavored with Italian bacon and combined with Fontina and mozzarella cheese make a delicious* timballo *when served with a velvety cherry-tomato-and-cream sauce. Fresh fava beans are usually available in the spring, but lima beans, either fresh or frozen, are a good alternative.*

**FOR THE SAUCE** *(makes 2 cups)*

1¾ pounds cherry tomatoes

1 tablespoon butter

½ cup heavy cream

½ cup freshly grated Parmigiano-Reggiano cheese

½ teaspoon salt

**FOR THE** *TIMBALLO*

Olive oil spray

2 large bay leaves

¼ pound pancetta, diced

4 to 6 quarts water

1 tablespoon salt

2½ cups shelled fresh fava or lima beans

1 pound farfalle

½ pound Fontina cheese, rind removed and diced

One ¼-pound fresh mozzarella cheese (*fior di latte*), diced

3 tablespoons half and half

Grinding of white pepper

Puree the cherry tomatoes in a food processor until smooth. Transfer the mixture to a fine mesh strainer over a bowl. Use a wooden spoon to press the tomato juice into the bowl; discard the seeds and skins. Alternately, use a food mill. There should be about 2¾ cups of tomato juice.

In a medium-size saucepan, melt the butter over medium heat. Pour in the tomato juice and cook, stirring, for a few minutes. Stir in the heavy cream, cheese, and salt and continue to stir until the ingredi-

ents are well blended. Reduce the heat to low and simmer the sauce, uncovered, until it is reduced by one third and thickens. Keep the sauce covered and warm while the *timballo* bakes.

Generously spray a 2½-quart ovenproof glass bowl or other similar mold with olive oil spray. Position the bay leaves in the base of the bowl and set aside.

Cook the pancetta in a medium-size nonstick pan over medium heat until the pancetta begins to crisp and give off its fat.

*continued*

Meanwhile, fill a pasta pot with an insert with the water and bring to a boil. Add the salt and fava or lima beans. Cook the beans until tender but not mushy. With a slotted spoon, remove the beans to a bowl, then add them to the pan with the pancetta. (Don't discard the water.) Cook the mixture over medium heat for 2 to 3 minutes. Set aside.

Preheat the oven to 350°F.

Add the farfalle to the boiling water, stir to prevent them from sticking, cover the pot, and bring the water back to a rolling boil. Uncover and cook the farfalle until *al dente*. Lift the insert and drain the pot, then return the farfalle to the pot. Over very low heat, stir in the pancetta mixture, the cheeses, half and half, and white pepper. When all the cheese has melted, transfer the mixture to the glass bowl, pressing down with a wooden spoon to compact it.

Cover the bowl tightly with a sheet of aluminum foil. Bake the *timballo* until browned on the bottom, 25 to 30 minutes. Remove the bowl from the oven and allow to cool for 10 minutes.

To unmold, remove the aluminum foil, place a serving dish over the top of the mold, and invert to unmold. Serve the *timballo* cut into wedges with sauce on the side.

NOTE: *The sauce can be made 2 days ahead, refrigerated, and then reheated.*

## PASTICCIO DI PASTA E FRUTTE DI MARE
# Seafood and Pasta Pie

MAKES ONE 9-INCH PIE

*During the Italian Renaissance, banquets became a feast for all the senses with an array of elaborately created dishes, some even gilded. One dish that gained special prominence in the city of Ferrara was the* pasticcio, *a slightly sweetened pastry crust pie containing pasta and meats, all blanketed in a velvety cream sauce. Today it is still a staple item on the menu of the Bar Centro Strorico, a modern café that is just across from the entrance to the beautiful pink-and-white marble facade of Ferrara's cathedral. For this interpretation of classic* pasticcio, *the pastry crust encases a seafood mixture of clams, scallops, cusk (a meaty, mild-flavored white fish that holds its shape), and shrimp with fettucine, though other types of pasta, both short- and long-cuts, can be used. Although this dish takes time to assemble, much of it can be done ahead. Make the pastry and line the springform pan a day ahead, make the besciamella sauce and refrigerate it a few days in advance, and rely on a ready supply of premade or store-bought pasta.*

### FOR THE PASTRY DOUGH
*(makes 1 pound 4 ounces)*

3 cups unbleached all-purpose flour

2 tablespoons sugar

1 teaspoon salt

6 tablespoons (¾ stick) butter, cut into small pieces

1 extra large egg, slightly beaten

¼ cup fresh lemon juice

2 to 3 tablespoons cold water, as needed

### FOR THE FILLING

2 dozen small fresh clams such as littleneck or mahogany clams, scrubbed and soaked in several changes of water (discard any with broken shells)

½ cup water or dry white wine for clams

3 cups water

½ pound small shrimp in the shell

½ pound firm fish fillets such as cusk or monkfish, cut into small pieces

½ pound sea scallops, cut in half

2 tablespoons fresh lemon juice

### FOR THE BESCIAMELLA SAUCE
*(makes 2 cups)*

¼ cup (½ stick) butter

¼ cup unbleached all-purpose flour

¼ cup reserved clam liquid

2 cups hot low-fat or whole milk

1 teaspoon fine sea salt

1 tablespoon grated lemon zest

½ pound fettucine, linguine, spaghetti, or other type pasta, homemade or store-bought

1 cup fresh or frozen peas

### FOR THE CRUST

1 large egg, slightly beaten

¼ teaspoon coarse sea salt

*continued*

Spray a 9 × 2-inch springform pan with vegetable spray and set aside.

In a food processor or a bowl, pulse or mix together the flour, sugar, and salt for the pastry dough. Add the butter and pulse or use a pastry blender until the butter is in tiny bits.

In a small bowl, whisk together the egg and lemon juice. In the food processor, pour the mixture through the feed tube with the motor running and allow the mixture to begin to form a ball of dough. Add the water a little at a time if the dough seems dry. Or add the liquid ingredients to the flour mixture in the bowl and use your hands to form a ball of dough.

Gather the dough into a ball, wrap in plastic wrap, and let it rest for 20 minutes or, if making it in advance, refrigerate it overnight.

When ready to use, roll 12 ounces (about three fifths) of the dough into a 16-inch circle on a lightly

*Making Seafood and Pasta Pie*

*Trimming the dough fitted into the springform pan.*

*Spreading the filling in the pan.*

*Covering the filling with the sheet of dough for the top crust.*

*Pinching and sealing together the dough for the top and bottom crusts.*

*Making a cut in the center of the top crust to vent steam that will build up while it is baking*

*Pasticcio di Pasta e Frutte di Mare (Seafood and Pasta Pie) (page 147)*

floured board. Lightly dust the top of the dough with flour then fold it into quarters, lift it, and unfold it to line the springform pan. Tuck it into the corners, bring the dough up the sides, and trim it so it is even with the top edge of the pan.

Roll the remaining dough out into a 12-inch circle and set aside, covered, until the filling is ready for the pan.

At this point, the dough-lined pan and the top crust can be refrigerated, covered, a day in advance of baking the *pasticcio*.

Place the clams in a large sauté pan, add the ½ cup water or wine, cover the pan, and cook over medium heat until the clams open. Discard any clams that do not open. Strain the clams with their juice through damp cheesecloth set over a bowl. When cool enough to handle, shuck the clams and transfer them to a large bowl. Strain the juice (about ¼ cup) and set aside.

In the same sauté pan, bring the 3 cups of water to a boil, add the shrimp, and cook them just until the shells turn color, about 1 minute. Drain the shrimp and when cool enough to handle, remove and discard the shells. Add the shrimp to the bowl with the clams, along with the cut-up fish and scallops. Pour the lemon juice over the fish and gently toss with a spoon. Set aside.

In a medium-size saucepan, melt the butter over medium heat; do not let it brown. Stir in the flour and whisk until smooth. Whisk in the reserved clam juice, then slowly whisk in the milk and continue whisking until the mixture thickens enough to coat a spoon. Stir in the salt and lemon zest. Cover and set aside. (The sauce can be cooled and refrigerated at this point; add a few drops of milk and reheat when ready to use as the sauce will thicken as it stands.)

Preheat the oven to 375°F. Cook the pasta according to the directions on page 30 for fresh pasta or page 29 for store-bought pasta. Add the peas and cook 1 minute before the pasta is done. Drain the pasta and peas into a colander and transfer the mixture to a large bowl. Carefully stir in the sauce and the seafood mixture.

Pour the ingredients into the springform pan. Cover the top with the second piece of dough, letting the edges overhang the pan. Trim the pastry edges and seal well. With a scissors cut a "v" or an an "x" in the center of the top crust. Brush the crust with the beaten egg and sprinkle with the coarse salt.

Bake the *pasticcio* until the crust is nicely browned, 45 to 50 minutes. Remove the pan to a cooling rack and allow to rest for 5 minutes before releasing the springform pan. Carefully transfer the *pasticcio* with the bottom of the springform pan to a serving dish. Cut into wedges and serve.

# Sweet Pastas

*Fettucine Dolci*
*(Sweet Pasta Ribbons)*

FETTUCINE DOLCI
# Sweet Pasta Ribbons

SERVES 4 TO 6

*Slightly sweet ribbons of fettucine puff up into randomly shaped coils and twists when they are deep-fried; then they are sprinkled with confectioners' sugar. Better make a double batch because these are habit-forming. This recipe might surprise you because it is pasta meant to be eaten as a sweet and is a distant cousin to the sweet pastas served during the Renaissance.*

1¾ cups unbleached all-purpose flour

½ cup finely ground semolina flour

1½ tablespoons granulated sugar

1 teaspoon ground cinnamon

¼ teaspoon ground cloves

3 large eggs

1 tablespoon grated lemon or orange zest

6 cups vegetable oil for frying

Confectioners' sugar

On a work surface, mix the flours, sugar, cinnamon, and cloves together. Fashion a *fontana* (page 9) and crack the eggs into the center. Add the lemon zest and with a fork break up and mix the eggs and zest together until smooth.

Use your hands and work in a clockwise fashion to bring the flour from the insides of the *fontana* into the egg mixture until it is thick. Keep mixing in flour until a rough ball of dough is formed. Push any excess flour aside and begin kneading the dough with your hands until it is smooth and not sticky. Add flour only if the dough is very tacky and soft.

Alternately make the dough in a food processor fitted with the steel blade. Add the eggs, granulated sugar, and zest to the work bowl and process to blend. Add the flours, cinnamon, and cloves and process until a ball of dough is formed. It will be slightly tacky. Remove the dough from the bowl and knead it on a floured surface until smooth, adding additional flour only if the dough is still sticky.

Let the dough rest covered under a bowl for 10 minutes to relax the gluten.

Divide the dough into four pieces and work with one piece at a time. Keep the remaining pieces covered. Roll and cut each piece as for fettucine (see page 11), except do not use the thinnest setting on the pasta machine. I find that this dough works best if it is thinned to a number 5 setting before it is cut into fettucine.

Heat the oil in a deep fryer or heavy-clad deep pot to 375°F. Drop a handful of fettucine at a time into the oil and fry until golden brown. Remove the fettucine with a slotted spoon to brown absorbent paper to drain.

Sprinkle the fettucine with confectioners' sugar and serve warm.

NOTE: *These freeze well unsugared in plastic containers for up to 3 months. Reheat in a low oven (325°F) for 5 minutes after defrosting, then sprinkle with the confectioners' sugar.*

*Torta di Tagliatelline di Modena (Modena's Classic Noodle Cake)*

TORTA DI TAGLIATELLINE DI MODENA

# Modena's Classic Noodle Cake

SERVES 8 TO 10

*The classic* torta di tagliatelline *(noodle cake) from Modena was known in the eighteenth century. The clever use of thinly cut uncooked pasta provides an interesting texture and look. The torta is best eaten the day it is made. Use a food processor to prepare the pastry and pasta doughs. Several other steps can be done the day before to save time; line the pan and have all the filling ingredients measured out. The tagliatelline, which are thinner than tagliatelle, should be made just before filling the pastry so they remain damp and are not brittle. Using a 9-inch pan will result in a slightly higher* torta, *but I prefer the thinner look achieved with a 10-inch pan.*

### FOR THE PASTRY DOUGH

1½ cups unbleached all-purpose flour

¼ cup plus 1 tablespoon sugar

½ teaspoon salt

5 tablespoons unsalted butter, cut into chunks

1 large egg

### FOR THE PASTA DOUGH FOR TAGLIATELLINE *(makes ½ pound)*

2 large eggs

1 cup plus 2 tablespoons unbleached all-purpose flour

⅛ teaspoon salt

### FOR THE FILLING

4 ounces slivered blanched almonds, processed to a powder

4 ounces mixed candied fruit peels, diced

2½ tablespoons sugar

2 tablespoons unsweetened cocoa powder

¼ cup (½ stick) unsalted butter, melted and cooled

2 large eggs

½ cup light cream

Butter a 9- or 10½ × 3-inch-deep springform pan, dust it with flour, and set aside.

For the pastry dough, place the flour, sugar, salt, and butter in the bowl of a food processor fitted with the metal blade and pulse until the butter is reduced to bits. Add the egg and process until the mixture begins to form a ball. Remove the dough from the work bowl, shape it into a disk, and wrap tightly in plastic wrap. Refrigerate at least 1 hour or overnight.

With a rolling pin, roll the pastry dough out on a floured surface into an 18-inch-diameter round and line the springform pan, bringing the dough 2 inches up the sides. Cover with plastic wrap and refrigerate until ready to use.

For the pasta dough, crack the eggs into the bowl of a food processor and pulse to break up. With the motor running, add the flour and salt. Allow the dough to form a ball that is moist but does not stick to your hands. If slightly sticky, do not add additional flour as the dough will be rolled out on a floured surface. If the dough appears too dry and crumbly, add a few drops of water.

Gather up the pasta dough and knead it on a lightly floured surface until it is soft and smooth, 3 to 4 minutes. Cover the dough with a bowl and let rest for 30 minutes while you make the filling.

In a medium-size bowl, mix the almonds, candied peels, sugar, and cocoa together. In a large bowl, whisk the butter, eggs, and cream together until blended. Stir the almond mixture into the butter mixture, blending well. Set aside.

Divide the pasta dough in half and work with one half at a time, keeping the piece you are not working with covered. Roll and cut the dough on a hand-crank pasta machine as described on page 11, using the vermicelli cut for the tagliatelline. Or roll and cut by hand as described on page 14. Lay the tagliatelline on floured kitchen towels as you make them, keeping them separated so that they do not clump together.

Preheat the oven to 350°F.

Scatter one third of the tagliatelline over the bottom of the pastry-lined springform pan. Carefully spread the filling over the top. Scatter the remaining tagliatelline evenly over the top of the filling. Cut a circle of parchment paper to fit the top of the pan. Butter the paper and place it over the top of the *torta*.

Bake until a cake skewer inserted into the center comes out clean and the pasta is golden brown, 30 to 35 minutes for a 10-inch pan and 35 to 40 minutes for a 9-inch pan. Halfway through the baking process, remove and discard the parchment paper. Transfer the *torta* to a cooling rack and cool completely before releasing the spring. Carefully slide the *torta* from the base onto a serving dish. Cut into thin wedges.

NOTE: *I find homemade candied peels far superior to store-bought. The recipe follows. Candied peels can be made several months in advance.*

## SCORZA D'ARANCIA CANDITA
# Candied Orange Peel

MAKES ABOUT 2 CUPS

*Even though you can purchase candied fruit peels in supermarkets and Italian specialty stores, the quality and taste just cannot compare, for my money, with the homemade version. The most popular is orange peel but the same procedure for making it can be used for lemon and grapefruit. Orange peel is called for in the exquisite-tasting Torta di Tagliatelline di Modena (see page 155). Candied peels can be made ahead and stored for months under refrigeration.*

3 large navel oranges, washed and dried

1½ cups water

1¼ cups granulated sugar

¼ teaspoon salt

⅔ cup turbinado (coarse brown) sugar

Cut the oranges in half and squeeze the juice; there should be about 1 cup. Set the juice aside. Cut each orange half in two and pull out the pulp and membranes. Using a very sharp small knife, scrape as much white pith as possible from the peel and discard it. Cut the peel into ¼-inch-wide strips. Place them in a medium-size saucepan and cover generously with cold water. Bring to a boil and boil for 1 minute. Drain the peel and rinse the saucepan. Repeat this process two more times. (Blanching the peel in boiling water helps to eliminate the bitterness.) Set the drained peel aside.

Pour the orange juice into a medium-size nonreactive saucepan and add the 1½ cups water, granulated sugar, and salt. Bring to a boil, stirring to dissolve the sugar. Add the blanched orange peel and stir the ingredients with a wooden spoon. Reduce the heat to low and simmer, uncovered, until the syrup thickens and reduces by about two thirds (it should be the consistency of corn syrup), about 2½ hours.

Spread the turbinado sugar in a 9 × 12-inch baking pan. Line a baking sheet with wax paper.

With a slotted spoon, remove the peel from the syrup and spread it over the turbinado sugar. With your fingers, roll the strips in the sugar to coat them evenly on all sides. Place the sugared strips on the baking sheet and let them dry, uncovered, overnight.

Store the candied peel in glass jars in the refrigerator or in glass jars or airtight plastic bags in the freezer.

TORTELLI DOLCI

# Sweet Tortelli

MAKES 5 DOZEN

*These sweet tortelli (ravioli) cookies have an unusual filling of ground chickpeas and* mostarda di frutta, *various whole candied fruits preserved in syrup, which usually accompanies boiled meats. The contrast of the bland chickpeas with finely diced fruit provides a nice flavor balance that is not too sweet. These cookies are a special treat at holiday time.*

**FOR THE DOUGH** *(makes 1½ pounds)*

2⅔ cups (11 ounces) unbleached all-purpose flour

1 teaspoon baking powder

5½ tablespoons butter

5 ounces granulated sugar (scant 1 cup)

1 large egg

2 tablespoons raspberry liqueur

1 tablespoon grated lemon zest (from 1 large lemon)

**FOR THE FILLING**

One 15-ounce can chickpeas, drained, rinsed, and patted dry

4 ounces *mostarda di frutta* or candied fruit

1 teaspoon ground cinnamon

3 teaspoons raspberry liqueur, or as needed

**TO FINISH**

Confectioners' sugar

Lightly butter two baking sheets and set aside.

In a large bowl, combine the flour and baking powder. In a medium-size bowl, beat the butter with the sugar until creamy. Beat in the egg and liqueur. Stir in the lemon zest.

Mix the butter mixture into the flour mixture and, with your hands, combine the ingredients into a dough. Remove the dough to a work surface and knead it for a few minutes, adding a little flour to the board if the dough is sticky. Do not make the dough too dry or it will be hard to roll. Let the dough rest, covered, while you make the filling.

In the bowl of a food processor, puree the chickpeas into a paste. Transfer the mixture to a bowl. Spray or oil a chef's knife and finely mince the candied fruit. Add the fruit to the chickpeas, stir in the cinnamon, and blend the ingredients well. If the mixture seems dry, add up to 3 teaspoons of raspberry liqueur. The mixture should have a paste consistency. Cover the filling and set aside.

Divide the dough into quarters and work with one quarter at a time, keeping the others covered. Roll the dough out with a rolling pin into a 12 × 10-inch rectangle. With a ruler and a butter knife, carefully measure out five rows of six 2-inch-square indentations. Do not cut through the dough. Place a generous teaspoon of the filling in the center of each square. Roll out a second piece of dough to the same dimensions and carefully place it on top of the filled squares.

With your hands gently press between the rows to seal the dough, then cut the squares with a pastry wheel and crimp the edges together with a fork dipped in flour.

Repeat with the remaining dough.

Preheat the oven to 350°F. Bake the tortelli until golden brown, 12 to 15 minutes. Transfer the tortelli to a cooling rack and sprinkle with confectioners' sugar when cool.

Store in airtight containers for up to 2 weeks.

NOTE: *If making the tortelli ahead, do not powder them with sugar until ready to serve.*

NOTE: *For a really special presentation, dust the tortelli with half confectioners' sugar and half sweetened cocoa powder (see photo below). To create the design, place a small triangular piece of wax paper diagonally on top of each tortello. Sprinkle the uncovered half with plain confectioners' sugar, and the other half with the cocoa powder.*

*Tortelli Dolci (Sweet Tortelli)*

# Mail-Order Sources

Balducci's
424 Avenue of the Americas
New York, NY 10011
800-Balducci Catalog
All kinds of Italian products: cheeses, pasta like fregola and maloreddus, olive oil

160Times
P.O. Box 236
South Berwick, ME 03908
www.ciaoitalia.com
Mail-order and Web site orders for *Ciao Italia* products, including personalized aprons, wooden dough scrapers, and wooden-pegged pasta forks, T-shirts

Claudio's King of Cheese
926 South Ninth Street
South Philadelphia, PA 19147
215-627-1873
Wide variety of Italian imported cheeses, pasta, prosciutto, olives, and olive oil

Colavita USA
2537 Brunswick Avenue
Linden, NJ 07036
800-665-4731 Catalog
Olive oil, pasta, balsamic vinegars, and gourmet gift selections

Dairy Fresh Candies
57 Salem Street
Boston, MA 02113
800-336-5536 Catalog
Candied citrus peels, complete line of shelled nuts, olive oils, balsamic vinegars, chocolates, and sweetened cocoa powders

Dean & DeLuca
Catalog Orders
P.O. Box 20810
Wichita, KS 67208-6810
800-221-7714
Italian meats, cheeses, olive oils, balsamic vinegars, and cookware

DiBruno Bros.
109 South Eighteenth Street
Philadelphia, PA 19103
215-665-9220 Catalog
Italian cheeses, dried meats, olives, pasta, and Del
Verde products

Draeger's
P.O. Box C
Menlo Park, CA 94026
800-642-9463
Cookware, cheese graters, rolling pins, and a complete
line of kitchenware

Fantes
1006 South Ninth Street
Philadelphia, PA 19147
800-878-5557
Pasta motor attachments, pasta machines, rolling pins,
cooking equipment, serving bowls, platters, and *chitarra*

Gallucci's Italian Foods
6610 Euclid Avenue
Cleveland, OH 44103
216-881-0045 Catalog
A complete Italian grocery store featuring cheeses,
olives, olive oils, pasta, vinegars, cured meats, sea salt,
and spices

Joe Pace and Son Grocer
42 Cross Street
Boston, MA 02113
617-227-9673 Catalog
Italian meats, cheeses, olive oils, olives, balsamic vinegars, pasta, anchovies, capers, and fine durum and
semolina flours

King Arthur Flour
P.O. Box 1010
Norwich, VT 05055
802-649-3881 Catalog
Semolina and durum flours, and unbleached all-
purpose flour

Kitchen Etc.
32 Industrial Drive
Exeter, NH 03833
800-232-4070 Catalog
Pasta pots, pasta machines, motors, attachments, rolling
pins, wooden boards, bowls, platters, and utensils

Pennsylvania Macaroni Company
2010-12 Penn Avenue
Pittsburgh, PA 15222
412-471-8330 Catalog
All types of pasta, olives, semolina and durum flours

San Francisco Herb Co.
250 Fourteenth Street
San Francisco, CA 94103
800-227-4530 Catalog
Complete line of spices, nuts, candied and citrus peels

The Spice Corner
904 South Ninth Street
Philadelphia, PA 19147
800-SPICES1 or 215-925-1661
Semolina flour, spices, and nuts

Zabar's
2245 Broadway
New York, NY 10024
212-787-2000 Catalog
Gadgets, kitchenware, cured meats, cheeses, cheesecloth, pasta pots, colanders, handle scoops, ravioli
forms, ravioli stamps, pastry wheels, and pastry brushes.

# Index